AUTHORED BY: RAS STRENGTH

THE LION'S ROAR

RASTAFARI LIVITY

A COMPREHENSIVE, CONCISE, DETAILED DESCRIPTION OF RASTAFARI WORSHIP & PRACTICES

Copyright © 2016 by Solomon & Makeda Publishing

All Rights Reserved. No Parts of this book may be reproduced in any form without the express written consent of Publisher/Author, except in the case of brief quotations embodied within relevant articles and book reviews for print and electronic media.

I Am A Rastafari

I Am A Rastafari! Nothing in this World is more clearer to I than that. It's not being Jamaican. It's not speaking Patois. It's not having locks. It's not even knowing Who and What H.I.M. Is! I Am Rastafari. Just like I have blood that looks red when the air hits it. Just like my skin is colored to protect I from some of My Brother Sun's rays. Just like my body temperature is balanced at 98.6 degrees, I Am Rastafari. It is something as difficult to explain to someone else as it would be to tell them what genetic chromosomes and proteins makes you who you are. And, I Know my brothers and sisters when I see them, hear them, interact with them in any way! I know the Vibrations, the Vibes, the Harmony, the Harmonics, the Spirit, the Soul of Rastafari that is INI Oneness. It is true that Rastafari is everywhere and in everyone, and it's just that ones express it a little, a little more, a lot more, all of it, and none. Rastafari Is Life! It's Iniverse! It's Union! It's Everything and All-things! Yes, there are those of INI who are to show and teach this way, bring it out of INI brothers and sisters, out of INI People! And So We Shall! Jah Rastafari Heights, Vibes, Love! Jah Bless INI!

Ras Jah Strength

Solomic Order, Emperor Menelik I Seal

Kabbalah's Tree of Life

The Order of Queen of Sheba

TABLE OF CONTENTS

The Emperors Listings..
Dedication...
Foreword...I
Preface...XI
The Introduction..XX
   Chapter 1: Word-Sound-Power..1
   Chapter 2: Word- Sound- Power: INI Theology...12
   Chapter 3: History of H.I.M..17
   Chapter 4: Rastafari Eldership/Timelines..31
   Chapter 5: The Nazirite Vow..35
   Chapter 6: Anointing & Oils..41
   Chapter 7: Houses And Mansions..48
   Chapter 8: The Hebraic Element..54
Interlude............................Omnify...64
   Chapter 9: The Applicable Hebraic Element..75
   Chapter 10: Requirements for Rastafari..82
   Chapter 11: What Is Man..97
   Chapter 12: The Ancient Nyabinghi Order {Structure}..........................101
   Chapter 13: Black Heights..116
   Chapter 14: Rastafari Prayers & Chants..127
Rastafari 50 Q & A...

Order of Queen of Sheba Seal "Guide and Index of World History, Dynasties and List of Rulers" for Ethiopia, Abyssinia"

Menelik I 204-179B.C.	Demahe 90-100
Handadyo 179-178	Autet 100-102
Auda Amat 178-167	Ella Auda 102-132
Auseyo 167-164	Zagan 132-136
Tzaue 164-133	Rema 132-136
Gasyo 133	Gafale 136-137
Mawat 133-125	Bese Zara 137-141
Bahas 125-116	Ella Azguagua 141-218
Qawda 116-114	Ela Harka 218-239
Qanaz 114-104	Bese Tzawetza 239-240
Haduna 104-95	Wakana 240
Wazba 95-94	Hadaus 240
Hadir 94-92	Ella Sagal 240-242
Kalas 92-85	Ella Asfeha I 242-256
Satyo 85-68	Ezanas I C250 AD
Filya 68-42	Ella Tzagab 256-279
Aglebu 42-39	Ella Samara 279-282
Ausena 39-38	Ella Aiba 282-298
Beriwas 38-9	Ella Eskendi 298-334
Mahsi 9-8	Ella Tzaham I 334-343
Be Sebazen 8 BC- 8AD	Ella San 343-356
Sartu 8-35	Ella Aiga 356-374
Laas 35-45	Ella Amida I 374-404
Masenh 45-52	**Ezanas II Bisi Halen 325-356
Setwa 52-61	Shizana 328-356
Adgala 61-71	Ella Abreha 356-370
Agba 71-73	Afred 370-374
Masis 73-77	Adhana I 374-379
Hakla 77-90	Rete'a 379-380

Asbeha 381-386	**Armah II, Ella Sahem, Ashama ibn Adjar 615-630
Ameda I 386-401	Germa Safar 633-648
Ella Shahe II 401-402	Zergaz 648-656
Gobaz I 402-404	Michael 656-677
Suhal 404-408	Baher Ikela 677-696
Abreha II 408-418	Hezba Seyon 696-720
Adhana II 418-424	Asagum 720-725
Yo'ab 424-434	Latem 725-741
Sahan 434-436	Tulatem 741-762
Ameda II 436-446	Adegos 762-775
Shahel II 446-448	Ayzur 775
Sabah 448-451	Dedem Almaz 775-790
Sahem 451-463	Wedemdem 780-790
Gobaz II 463-474	Demawedem 790-820
Agabe 474-475	Rema Armah III 820-825
Levi 474-475	Degnajan II 825-846
Ella Amida (IV)? 475-486	Del Nead 905-950
Jacob I 486-489	**Zegwe Dynasty**
David 486-489	Mara Tekle Haimanot 916-919
Armah I 489-504	Tatadim 919-959
Zitana 504-505	Jan Seiyoum 959-999
Jacob II 505-514	Germa Seiyoum 999-1039
**Caleb, Ella Asbena, El Eshaba 514-542	St. Yemrehana Christos 1039-1079
King in Yeman 523-525	St. Harbe 1079-1119
Beta Israel 542-550	St. Gebra Maskal Lalibela 1119-1159
Gabra Masqal 550-564	St. Na'akuto Le'Ab 1159-1207
Constantine 564-578	Yetbarek 1207-1247
Wason Sagad 578-591	Mairari 1247-1262
Feresanay 591-601	Harbe II 1262-1270
Adreaz 601-623	
Eklewudem 623-633	

Solomonic Dynasty	Lebna Kengel (David II) 1508-1540
Yekuno Amlak, Tasfa Iyasus or St. Tekle Haimanot 1207-1285	**Galawedos (Claudius) 1540-1559
Solomon I 1285-1294	Menas 1560-1564
Bahr Asgad 1294-1297	Sarsa Dengel 1564-1597
Senfa Asgad 1294-1297	Jacob 1597-1603, 1604-1607
Hezba Asgad 1295-1296	Za Dengel 1603-1604
Qedma Asgad 1296-1297	Susneyos (Sissinios) 1607-1632
Jin Asgad 1297-1298	Fasilidas (Basllides) 1632-1666
Saba Asgad 1297-1298	Yohannes (John) I 1667-1682
Wedem Arad 1299-1314	Iyaso (Jesus) I the Great 1682-1706
Amda Siyon (Seyio) I 1314-1344	Tekle Haimanot I 1706-1708
Newaya Krestos 1344-1372	Na'od II 1708-d 1722
Newaya Maryam 1372-1382	Tewoflos (Theophilus) 1708-1711
Dawit (David) I 1382-1411	Yostos (Justus) 1711-1716
Tewodros (Theodore) I 1411-1414	Dawit (David) III 1716-1721
Isaac 1414-1429	Walda George 1721
Andrew 1429-1430	Asma George Bekaffa 1721-1730
Takla Maryam 1430-1433	Iyous (Joas) II 1730-1755
Zara Yakob (Constantine I) 1434-1468	Iyous (Joas) I 1755-1769
Baeda Mariam I 1468-1478	Yohannes II 1769
Constantine II 1478-1484	Tekle Haimanot II 1769-1777
Amda Seyon II 1494-(1484)	Salomon (Solomon) II 1777-1779
Na'od 1494 (1484)-1508	

Tekle Giorgis (George) I 1779-1784, 1788-1789, 1794-1795, 1795-1796, 1796-1799, 1800, d 1817	Yohannes IV of Tigre 1871-1884, Egyptions defeated, driven out of Eritrea, Battle of Gundet, 1875, Battle of Gura, 1876
Jesus III 1784-1788	Menelik (Menilek) II 1868, 1889-1913, Italians defeated at Battle of Adwa 1896 Etege T'aytu Bet'ul regent 1910
Ba'eda Maryam I 1788	Ras Tesemma regent 1910-1911
Hezekia 1789-1794	Lij Iyasu (Joshua), Jesus V regent 1912-1913, Emperor 1913-1916, d 1935
Ba'eda Maryam II 1795	Zawditu Empress 1916-1930
Solomon III 1796-1797-1799	Haile Selassie (Sellassie) Ras Tafari Makonnen regent 1916-1930, Emperor 1930-1936, 1941-1974
Jonah 1797-1798, d 1832	Asta Wossen Amha Selassie 1974-1975 d 1997 Aman Mikael Andom Head of State 1974
Demetrius 1799-1800, 1800-1801, d 1803	Tafari Benti 1974-1977
Egwala Seyon 1801-1818	
Joas II 1818-1821	Mengistu Haile Mariam 1977-1987, President 1987-1991
Gigar 1821-1826, 1826-1830, d 1831	Meles Zenawi 1991-1995
Ba'eda Maryam III 1820	Negasso Gidada 1995-2001
Jesus IV 1830-1832	Girma Wolde-Giorgis 2001-Present
Gabra Krestos 1832,1832	
Sahla Dengel 1832, 181832-1840, 1841-1845, 1845-1850, 1851-1855	
Yohannes III 1840-1841, 1845, 1850-1851, d. 1865	
Ali Alula 1851-1853	
Tewodros (Theodore) II 1855-1868, Takes diplomats hostage, British Expedition, defeat and Suicide of Tewodros, 1868	
Tekle Giogris II of Zagwe 1868-1871	

Color Key:

==**Ezanas II Bisi Halen (First Coptic Bishop 305) stela erected at Juncture of Nile & Atbara.==

Caleb, Ella Asbena, el Eshaba : At Roman urging, Ethiopians install a Christian King in Yeman

Armah II, Ella Sahem, Ashama ibn Adjar : Traditional King who welcomed Muslim refugees from Mecca.

Galawedos (Claudius) : Moslems allied to Turkey defeated, with Portuguese help, Battle of Lake Tana 1543

Charles Rey's "The Real Abyssinia" by Seeley Service & Co. 1935, List of Emperors of Ethiopia

IV. MENELIK I SOLOMONIC DYNASTY:
BCE
1. Menelik I 957 2. Hanyon 956 3. Sera I (Tomai) 930 4. Amen Hotep Zagdur 899 5. Aksumay Ramissu 879 6. Awseyo Sera II 841 7. Tawasya II 820 8. Abralyus Wiyankihi II 788 9. Aksumay Warada Tsahay 765 10. Kashta Hanyon 752 11. Sabaka II 740 12. Queen Nicauta Kandake 13. Tsawi Terhak Warada Nagash 681 14. Erda Amen Awseya 675 15. Gasiyo Eskikatir ? 16. Nuatmeawn 671 17. Tomadyon Piyankihi III 659 18. Amen Asero 643 19. Piyankihi IV (Awtet) 609 20. Zaware Nebret Aspurta 568 21. Saifay Harsiataw II 556 22. Ramhay Nastossanan 542 23. Handu Wuha Abra 531 24. Safelya Sabakon 500 25. Agalbus Sepekos 478 26. Psmenit Waradanegash 457 27. Awseya Tarakos 445 28. Kanaz Psmis (son of preceding) 432 29. Apras 422 30. Kashta Walda Ahuhu 402 31. Elalion Taake 392 32. Atserk Amen III 382 33. **Atserk Amen IV** 372 34. Queen Hadina 362 35. Atserk Amen V 352 36. Atserk Amen VI 342 37. Queen Nikawla Kandat 332 38. Bassyo 325 39. Queen Akawsis Kandake III 315 40. Arkamen II 305 41. Awtet Arawura 295 42. Kolas II (Kaletro) 285 43. Zawre Nebrat 269 44. Stiyo 255 45. Safay 242 46. Queen Nikosis Kandake IV 232 47. Ramhay Arkamen IV 222 48. Feliya Hernekhit 207 49. Hende Awkerara 187 50. Agabu Baseheran 177 51. Sulay Kawawmenun 157 52. Messelme Kerarmer 149 53. Nagey Bsente 139 54. Etbenukawer 129 55. Safeliya Abramen 109 56. Sanay 99 57. Queen Awsena 88 58. Dawit II 78 59. Aglbul 70 60. Bawawl 60 61. Barawas 50 62. Dinedad 40 63. Amoy Mahasse 35 64. Nicotnis Kandake V 25 65. Nalke 20 66. Luzay 8 67. **Bazen** *BCE YEAR 8 to AD YEAR 9*

Non-Christian Rulers After Christian Era (AD):
1. Sartu Tsenfa Assegd 30 2. Akaptah Tsenfa Ared 38 3. Horemtaku 40 4. Garsemot Kandake VI 50 5. Hatosza Bahr Asaged 78 6. Mesenh Germasir 85 7. Metwa Germa Asfar 94 8. Adgale II 104 9. Agba 6 mo of Adgale + 6 mo 105 10. Serada 121 11. Malis Alameda 125 12. Hakabe Nasohi Tsiyon 131 13. Hakli Sergway 143 14. Dedme Zaray 153 15.

Awtet 155 16. **ALaly Bagamay** 162 17. **Awadu Jan Asagad** 192 18. **Zagun Tsion Hegez** 197 19. **Rema Tsion Geza** 200 20. **Azegan Malbagad** 207 21. **Gafale Seb Asagad** 208 22. **Tsegay Beze Wark** 212 23. **Gaza Agdur** 221 24. **Agduba Asgwegwe** 229 25. **Dawiza** 230 26. **Wakana** (Queen) 2 days 27. **Hadawz** 4 months 28. **Ailassan Sagal** 233 29. **Asfehi Asfeha** 247 30. **Atsgaba Seifa Arad** 253 31. **Ayba** 270 32. **Tsaham Laknduga** 279 23. **Tsegab** 289 34. **Tazer** 299 35. **Ahywa Sofya** (Queen) 306 . The line continues with Christian rulers and Ethiopia becomes a Christian nation.

Christian Rulers After Christian Era (AD):
1. **Ahywa** (Sofya, mother of Abreha Atsbeha). 2. **Abreha Atsbeha** (partly with his mother) 332 3. **Atsbeha** (alone) 344 4. **Asfeh Dalz** 351 5. **Sahle** 365 6. **Arfed Gebra Maskal** 369 7. **Adhana I** (Queen) 374 8. Riti 375 9. **Asfeh II** 376 10. **Atsbeha II** 381 11. **Amey** 396 12. **Abreha II** 7 months 13. Ilassahl 2 months 14. **Elagabaz I** 398 15. Suhal 402 16. **Abreha III** 412 17. **Adhana II** (Queen) 418 18. **Yoab** 428 19. **Tsaham I** 430 20. **Amey II** 431 21. **Sahle Ahzob** 433 22. **Tsebah Mahana Kristos** 436 23. **Tsaham II** 438 24. **Elagabaz II** 444 25. **Agabi** 445 26. **Lewi** 447 27. **Ameda III** 450 28. **Armah Dawit** 464 29. **Amsi** 469 30. **Salayba** 478 31. **Alameda** 486 32. **Pazena Ezana** 493 . Kaleb continues the line as a Dynasty until Emperor Gedajan.

Kaleb Dynasty:
1. **Kaleb** 523 2. **Za Israel** 1 month 3. **Gabra Maskal** 537 4. **Kostantinos** 565 5. **Wasan Sagad** 580 6. **Fere Sanay** 603 7. **Advenz** 623 8. **Akala Wedem** 631 9. **Germa Asafar** 646 10. **Zergaz** 656 11. **Dagena Mikael** 682 12. **Bahr Ekla** 701 13. **Gum** 725 14. **Asguagum** 730 15. **Latem** 746 16. **Talatam** 767 17. **Gadagosh** 780 18. **Aizar Eskakatir** 1/2 day 19. **Dedem** 785 20. **Wededem** 795 21. **Wudme Asfare** 825 22. **Armah** 830 23. **Degennajam** 849 24. **Gedajan** 850 25. **Gudit** (Yodit, a Jewish Queen) 890 26. **Anbase Wedem** 910 27. **Del Naad** 920 . Events ends Solomonic dynasty and begins the Zagwe (line of Moses) Dynasty

V. ZAGWE Dynasty

1. **Mara Takla Haymanot** (Zagwe) 933 2. **Tatawdem** 973 3. **Jan Seyum** 1013 4. **Germa Seyum** 1053 5. **Yermrhana Kristos** 1093 6. **Kedus Arbe** (samt) 1133 7. **Lalibala** 1173 8. **Nacuto Laab** 1213 9. **Yatbarak** 1230 10. **Mayrari** 1245 11. **Harbay** 1253

(Israelite rulers during Zagwe Dynasty: 1. **Mahbara Wedem** 2. **Agbea Tsion** 3. **Tsinfa Arad** 4. **Nagash Zare** 5. **Asfeh** 6. **Yacob** 7. **Bahr Asagad** 8. **Edem Asagad**).

Yekuno Amlak throned and continues the Solomonic line.

VI. YEKUNO AMLAK AND HIS SOLOMONIC POSTERITY

1. **Yekuno Amlak** 1268 2. **Yasbeo Tseyon** 1277 3. **Tsenfa Arad** 1278 4. **Hesba Asagad** 1279 5. **Kedme Asagad** 1280 6. **Jan Asagad** 1281 7. **Sabea Asagad** 1282 8. **Wedma Ared** 1297 9. **Amda Tseyon** 1327 10. **Saifa Ared** 1355 11. **Wedma Asfare** 1365 12. **Dawit** 1395 13. **Tewodoros** 1399 14. **Yeshak** 1414 15. **Andreyas** 6 months 16. **Hesba Nafi** 1418 17. **Bedl** Nafi (6 mo with Andreyas) 1419 18. **Amde Tseyon** 1426 19. **Zara Yacob** 1460 20. **Boeda Maryam** 1470 21. **Iskender** 1486 22. **Amda Tseyon** 1487 23. **Naod** 1500

24. **Lebna Dengel** 1532 25. **Galawdewos** 1551 26. **Minas** 1555. The Emperors and Empresses moved around the realm until the establishment of Gonder as a Capital City. The line continues as House of Gondar.

VII. THE HOUSE OF GONDAR

1. **Sartsa Dengel** 1589 2. **Yakob** 1598 3. **Za Dengel I** 1599 4. **Susneyos** 1627 5. **Fasil** 1662 6. **Degu-Johannis** 1677 7. **Adyam Sagad Iyasu** 1702 8. **Takla Haymanot** 1704 9. **Tewoflus** 1707 10. **Yostos** 1711 11. **Dawit** 1716 12. **Bakaffa** 1725 13. **Birhan Sagad Iyasu** 1749 14. **Iyoas** 1764 15. **Johannis** 5 months + 5 days 16. **Takla Haymanot** 1772 17. **Solomon** 1774 18. **Takla** Giyorgis 1779. The accession line continues by Princes who claimed the throne as Emperors. These Princes began the Zemene Mesafint Era.

VIII. RULERS of ZEMENE MESAFINT ERA

1. **T. Yasus** 1784-88 2. **Takla Haymanot** 1788-89 3. **Iskias** 1789-95 4. **Baeda Maryam** 1795- 97 5. **Junus** 1797 6. **Adimo** 1797-99 7. **Egwala Sion** 1799-1818 8. **Joas** 1818-21 9. **Gigar** 1821-26 10. **Baeda Maryam III** 1826 11. **Gigar** (again) 1826-30 12. **Iyasu IV** 1830-32 13. **Gabra Kristos** 1832 14. **Sahala Dengel** 1832-40 15. **Johannes III** 1840-41 16. **Sahala Dengel** (again) 1841-55 . The end of Zemene Mesafint begins with Tewodros.

IX. RULERS of MODERN ETHIOPIA

1. **Theodore** 1855-68 2. **John IV** 1868-89 3. **Menelik II** 1889-1913 6. **Lej Yasu** 1913-16 7. **Zauditu** (Empress) & **Ras Tafari Makonnen** (Regent & Heir) 1916 **Negus Tafari Makonnen** (King) 1928-1930 8. **Haile Selassie I** 1930-1974. The Royal line is terminated by Marxist and Tribalist Unknowns

X. SOLOMONIC LINE DISRUPTED BY REVOLUTIONARIES

1. Communist and Ethnic-oriented leaders reversed the continuity of the Solomonic line.

Dedication

The Lion's Roar is Dedicated to I Wife, Queen Empress Makeda Nana Gordon. You Have "Lifted I Life" and "Brightened I Light" of Jah Rastafari More than I Knew Possible! You Have Given I "The Oneness" that Rastafari Is. You Have Proved "Divine Love" that Rastafari Teaches. You Have Given I "The Fullness" that Rastafari Expresses. And, You Have Made INI Mystical Marriage Ascend INI Soul and Spirit and Manifest into INI Flesh and Bones! Jah Rastafari, His Imperial Majesty Haile Selassie 1st, Is INI I Love.

Foreword

Rastafari Is A Way Of Life. It's a way of Life because religion has become the imprisonment of the human soul and psyche. Religion restricts, limits, confines, and does not allow for the expression of a liberated mind. Religion is dangerous, and a threat, to the growth and development of life. Let I explain why:

The existence of religion is rooted fundamentally in human ignorance. People do not know the origin of the world, why there is death, or the answers to other basic questions. Explanations must be devised on the basis of a complete lack of evidence. The first concepts of these came to InI Ancient Ancestors in Kemet, Alkebulan. They were expressed in ways that are profoundly obscure to the Western Mind, so they had to make sense of it. The first Western explanations gave the world the fascinating mythologies of the Ancient Greeks, Romans, and other civilizations. Under the influences of Judaism and Christianity, mythology was replaced, in Western Civilization, by religions based on pseudo-historical events. Afterwards, all acceptances of religion became based on belief, not on the weight of evidence, or the reaching of reasonable conclusions by insight, contemplation, or meditation.

This means, as a result, that all statements about God or the gods are statements of belief. Even the assertion that there is no God, Atheism, is a statement of belief. In the case of religions based on historical events, interpretations of those events, and their deities, are accepted by believers as true. Nonbelievers arrive at completely different interpretations.

If belief is the key to religion, it is also the chief problem. If religion were a form of knowledge, then its teachings would have to be supported by visible evidence that could be examined by anyone. There would then be widespread acceptance of it as knowledge as there is in mathematics or the natural sciences. But there can be no evidence, as science understands the term, that a supreme being created the universe. Nor can there be any evidence of life after death. These and other beliefs are not open to verification; they are matters of study, evaluation, elevation, and faith. So, One has to trust that they are true; but they do seem to give valid explanations to fundamental questions.

It has been said that thoughts of death are what lead necessarily to the development of religion. It is difficult to imagine what need there would be for religion in a world in which no one ever died or became ill. So religion's attempt to give answers to these basic questions: From where did the world come; What is the meaning of human life; Why do people die and what happens afterward; Why is there evil; And how should people behave; started out as a comforting of the mind, with good intentions. As is stated above, in the distant past these questions were answered in terms of mythology. Now, much literature deals with them, and the modern sciences try to investigate them.

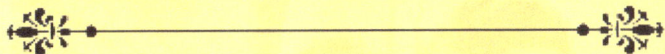

As a word, religion is difficult to define, and as a human experience, it seems to be a universally complex subject of inquiry and research. The 20th-century German-born American Theologian Paul Tillich gave a simple and basic definition of the word: "Religion is Ultimate Concern." This means that religion encompasses that to which people are most devoted or that from which they expect to get the most fundamental satisfaction in life. Consequently, religion does provide adequate answers to the basic questions posed above.

Four centuries earlier, the German Reformer Martin Luther spoke in similar terms about God. He stated that to have a god was to "have something in which the heart trusts completely," whether such a god was a supernatural being or something in the world like wealth, power, career, or pleasure, made no difference. Putting Tillich's and Luther's definitions together, it is possible to see that religion does not necessarily have to be involved with shrines, temples, churches, or synagogues. It does not need complex doctrines or clergy. It can be anything to which people devote themselves, that fills their lives with relative meaning.

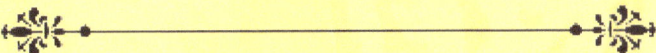

In Western Civilization, religion has traditionally been defined as belief in and worship of one God. This is true for Judaism, Christianity, and Islam. The statement by Tillich and Luther make it clear, however, that such a definition may be too narrow. In original Buddhism in India and Confucianism in China, there was no recognition of a supreme being. Both of these philosophies were basically concerned with patterns in human behavior. Rastafari is a metaphysical combination of all of these, and more than any one of them. It is ambiguous in nature because of the individual needs that arise from the spiritual minded.

Regardless of definitions, all religions (as the word is normally used) have certain elements in common. These include common rituals to perform, prayers to recite, places to frequent or avoid, holy days to keep, means by which to predict the future, a body of literature to read and study, truths to affirm, charismatic leaders to follow, and ordinances to obey. Many have buildings set aside for worship, and there are activities such as prayer, sacrifice, contemplation, and perhaps a form of magic. Most of these tenants are present in Rastafari, depending on the various houses or mansions; but they are done in a connective way, a oneness of value. This inclusiveness raises the accomplishments that Rastafari can bring forth out of any individual.

Closely associated with these elements is personal conduct. Although it is possible to separate ritual observances from moral conduct, worship has normally implied a type of relationship with a god from which certain behavior patterns are expected to be followed. A notable exception in history is the official state religion of Ancient Rome, which was kept separate from personal commitment and morality. This is why a Theocratic Ivernment has always been better suited to serve a nation.

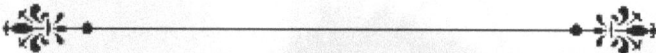

Narrowly understood, religion means actions, especially cultic or ceremonial, that express reverence for the gods. The usual Greek word for this is Threskeia, meaning "religious zeal" and "Worship of God," but can also have a negative sense when used of deviant or suspect cults.

More broadly, religion involves a complex of faith and conduct. For this, the common Greek term is Eusebeia, "piety," that is, reverence for the gods and for the social or moral order, which they uphold. Threskeia and Eusebeia are deeply present in the Rastafari Man and Wombman. This is why there is a Permeation of Spiritual Livity for InI.

Theological conclusions are sometimes drowned from the huge amounts of linguistic evidence explaining the contexts of religion; within its narrative. The relative rarity of words for "religion" in the Bible, and the confining of the broader terms in what are generally considered the latest writings of the New Testament, and modern theological commentaries, have been used to argue that "religion," with its connotations of outward activity or generalized piety, is an inappropriate language to use for Ancient Israel or of earliest Christianity, which is why Rastafari avoids using the term as a title of Rastafari Livity. "Faith", as the inner response to God's call, would be more proper. To use the term "religion" of the Pentateuch, Christian liturgical services, and Islamic Hadiths and/or Sunnahs, is, however, appropriate, since there is that correct performance of cultic activity, as well as ethical duty, and is essential in Jewish's, Western Christianity's, and Sunni/Shite Islam's response and devotion to God.

IV

The Ancient Greeks speculated on the meaning of religion, as evident in the writings of Plato and Aristotle. The people of the Bible wrote about religious experiences. But the Psychology of Religion, in a technical sense, could not arise until psychology itself became a discipline apart from philosophy. This occurred with studies and experiments that pointed out the Neuropsychological evidence of an unseen element affecting the observable.

This observable reaction to the unseen is described as "Religious Experience", and is explained in the various sections of many commentaries of the Holy Books. Scholars have written thousands of exegeses on specific experiences like wonder at the infinity of the cosmos, the sense of awe and mystery in the presence of the holy, feelings of dependence on a divine power or an unseen order, the sense of guilt and anxiety accompanying belief in a divine judgment, and the feeling of peace that follows faith in divine forgiveness, among many other sub-topics. Some thinkers also point to a religious aspect of the purpose of life and with the destiny of the individual.

In a first sense, Religious Experience means an encounter with other persons and/or things in this world that inspires. In other words, encounters with the Divine is as real as anything we know of; when a sense of awe is obtained through an object of sacred reverence.

In a second case, reference is made not to an encounter with a divine being but rather to the apprehension of a quality of Holiness or Rightness in Reality, or the fact that all experiences can be viewed in relation to the ground from which they spring. In short, Religious Experience means both special experience of the Divine or Ultimate and the viewing of any experience as pointing to the Divine or Ultimate.

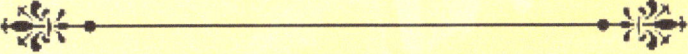

Religious Experience must be understood against the background of a general theory of experience as such. Experience, as conceived from the standpoint of a British Philosophical Tradition, stemming from John Locke and David Hume, is essentially the reports of the world received through the senses. Experience, as a tissue of sensible content, was set in contrast to reason, which was understood as the domain of logic and mathematics. The Mind was envisaged as a wax tablet on which the sensible world imprints itself, and the One who experiences is the passive recipient of what is given. It is possible to distinguish and compare these sensible items by means of overstanding them as concepts, but the depth themselves are available only through experience-i.e., the sensation of things and reflections upon thought and mental activities, feelings, and desires. According to this Empiricist view, all ideas, beliefs, and theories, expressed in conceptual form, are to be traced back to their origin, if they are to be understood and justified.

Rastafari is gaining more intellectual and theological academia that clarifies InI state and standard. As a result, InI can point out how the above view of experience came under criticism from two sides.

Immanuel Kant, an 18th-century German Philosopher, who still retained some of the assumptions of the position he criticized, nevertheless declared that experience is not identical with passively received sensible material but must be construed as the joint product of such material; and it's being grasped by an understanding that thinks in accordance with certain necessary categories may not be derived from the senses. Kant opened the way for a new understanding of the element of interpretation in all experience, and his successors in the development of German Idealism, Johann Fichte, Friedric Schelling, and G.W.F. Hegel, came to characterize experience as the many-sided reflection of man's multiple encounters with the world, other men, and himself.

A second attack on the classical conception came from U. S. Pragmatist Philosophers, notable Charles Sanders Peirce, William James, and John Dewey, for whom experience was the medium for the disclosure of whatever there is to be encountered; it is far richer and more complex than a passive registry of sensible data. Experience was seen as a human activity related to the purposes and interests of the one who experience, and it was understood as an interpreted product of multiple transactions between man and the environment. Moreover, stress was placed on the social and funded character of experience in place of the older conception of experience as a private content confined to the mind of an individual. On this view, experience is not confined to its contents but includes modes or dimensions that represent frames of meaning; social, moral, aesthetic, political, religious, through which whatever that is encountered can be interpreted. James went beyond his associates in developing the broadest theory of experience, known as Radical Empiricism, according to which; the relations and connections between items of experience are given along with these items themselves.

Critics of the classical view of experience, while not concerned exclusively with Religious Experience, saw, nevertheless, that if experience is confined to the domain of the senses it is then difficult if the Divine is not also regarded as one sensible object among others. This consideration prompted attempts to Overstand experience in a broader term. Cutting across all theories of experience is the basic fact that experience demands expression in language and symbolic forms. To know what has been experienced, and how it is to be Overstood, requires the ability to identify things, persons, and events through naming, describing, and interpreting; which involve appropriate concepts and language. No experience can be the subject of analysis while it is being had or undergone. Communication and critical inquiry require that experience be cast into a symbolic form that arrests them for further scrutiny. The various uses of language, political affiliation, scientific knowledge, moral aptitude, and religious belief, represent multiple purposes through which experience is described and interpreted.

Specifically, religious experience has been variously identified in the following ways: the Awareness of the Holy, which evokes awe and reverence; the feeling of absolute dependence that reveals man's status as a creature; the sense of being At One with the Divine; the Perception of an unseen order or of a quality of "Permanent Rightness" of the Cosmic Scheme; the Direct Perception of God; the encounter with a reality "wholly other"; and the sense of a Transforming Power as a presence. Sometimes, as in the striking case of the Old Testament Prophets, the experience of God has been seen as Critical Judgment on man. And as the disclosure of His dimension or aspect of experience point to man's attitude toward an overarching ideal, to a total reacting to life, to an ultimate concern for the meaning of one's being, or to a quest for a power that integrates human personality, his Overstanding is Elevated. In all these cases, it is the fact that the attitudes and concerns in question are directed to an Ultimate Object, beyond man, that justifies their being called religious. All interpreters have agreed that Religious Experience involves what is final in value to man and concerns belief in what is Ultimate in Reality, and in this regard Rastafari also agrees.

Because of their intimate relation to one another, the religious and the moral have often been confused. The problem has been intensified by many attempts, beginning with Kant's treatise on religion (1793), that interprets religion as essential morality or merely as an incentive for doing one's duty. Religion and morality are, however, usually taken to be distinguishable. Religion concerns the being of a person, what he is and what he acknowledges as the worshipful reality, while morality concerns what the person does and the principles governing his relation to others. While it is generally acknowledged that religion must affect man's conduct in the world, some have maintained that there is no morality without religion, while others deny this claim on the grounds that morality must remain Autonomous and "Free" of "Divine Sanctions". Since it is concerned with the Holy and Purpose of Human Life as a whole, most scholars would hold that Religious Experience should be related, in an intelligible way, to all other experiences and forms of experiences, including those that are concerned with or construct morality. The task of tracing out these relationships belongs to Theology and the Philosophy of Religion. For Rastafari, religion doesn't affect man's conduct absolutely, but there can't be any morality without a type of Divine Presence and Structure.

Religious Experience may be distinguished from the aesthetic aspect of experience in that the former involves commitment and devotion to the Divine, while the latter is focused on the appreciation and enjoyment of qualities, forms, and patterns in themselves, whether as natural objects or works of art. Anthropological studies have shown that Primitive Religions gave birth to many forms of art that, in the course of development, won independence as secular forms of expression. The problem in the relation between religion and art is posed in a particularly acute way when reference is made to religious art as a special form of the aesthetic.

All Religious Experience can be described in terms of three basic elements: first, the personal concerns, attitudes, feelings, and ideas of the individual who has the experience; second, the religious object disclosed in the experience or the reality of which it is said to refer; and third, the social forms that arise from the fact that the experience in question can be shared. Although the first two elements can be distinguished for purposes of analysis, they are not separated within the integral experience itself. Religious Experience is always found in connection with a personal concern and quest for the Real Self, oriented towards the power that makes Life Holy, or a ground and a goal of all existence. A wide variety of individual experiences are thus involved, among which are attitudes of seriousness and solemnity, in the face of the mystery of human destiny; feelings of awe and of being unclean, evoked by the encounter with the holy; the sense of a power or a person who both loves and judges man; the experience of being converted or of having the Course of Life directed towards the Divine; the feeling of relief stemming from the sense of Divine forgiveness; the sense that there is an unseen order or power upon which the value of all Life depends; and finally, the sense of being At One with the Divine and of abandoning the egocentric self.

VIII

In all these situations, the experience is realized in the Life of an individual who, at the same time, has his attention focused on an "other," or Divine Reality, that is present or encountered. The determination of the nature of this "other" poses a problem of interpretation that requires the use of symbols, analogies, images, and concepts, for expressing the reality that evokes a religious experience in an understandable way. Four basic conceptions of the Divine may be distinguished: the Divine as an impersonal, sacred order (Logos, Tao, Rta Asha) governing the universe and man's destiny; the Divine as power that is Holy and must be approached with awe, proper preparation, or ritual cleansing; the Divine as an All-Embracing One, the Ultimate Unity and Harmony of all finite realities and the goal of the Mystical Quest; and the Divine as an Individual or Self; Transcending the world, and man, and yet standing in relation to both; at the same time.

The two most important concepts, that have been developed by theologians and philosophers, for the interpretation of the Divine are Transcendence and Immanence. Each is meant to express the relation between the Divine and finite realities. Transcendence means going beyond the limit or surpassing a boundary. Immanence means remaining within or existing within the confines of a limit. The Divine is said to transcend man and the world when it is viewed as distinct from both and not wholly identical with either. The Divine is also said to be imminent when it is viewed as wholly or partially identical with some reality within the world, such as man or the cosmic order. The conception of the Divine as an impersonal, sacred, order, represents the extreme of immanence; since the order is regarded as entirely within the world and not as imposing itself from without. The conception of the Divine as an Individual or Self represents the extreme of transcendence since God is taken as not wholly identical with either the world or any finite reality within it. Some thinkers have described the Divine as wholly transcendent of or "wholly other" than finite reality, some have maintained the total Immanence of the Divine, and still, others claim that both concepts can be applied, and therefore, that the two characteristics do not exclude each other.

Religious Experience is always Overstood by those who have it as pointing beyond themselves to some reality regarded as Divine. For the believer, Religious Experience discloses something other than self; this referent is sometimes described as the "Intentional Object" that is meant or aimed at by the experiencing person. Analysis of Religious Experience, interpretations placed upon it, and the beliefs to which it gives rise, may result in the denial that there is any such reality to be encountered or that the assertion of it is justified by the experience in question. This is not a conclusion however, and does not change the fact that all Religious Experience, whether that of the mystic who strives for Unity with God or of the naturalist who points to a religious quality in life, purports to be the experience "of" something other than itself.

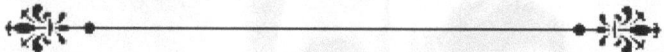

The question of the Cognitive Import or the Objective Validity of Religious Experience is one of the most difficult problems encountered in the Philosophy of Religion. In confronting the question, it is necessary to distinguish between various ways of describing the phenomena under consideration and the critical appraisal of "Truth Claims" concerning the reality of the Divine; made on the basis of these phenomena. Even if describing and appraising are not utterly distinct, and involve one another, it is generally admitted that the question of validity cannot be settled on the basis of historical or descriptive accounts alone. Validity and Cognitive Import are matters calling for logical, semantic, epistemological, and metaphysical criteria, of the principles of rational order and coherence; meaning, Knowledge and Reality; and this means that the appraisal of Religious Experience is ultimately a philosophical and theological problem. But the anthropologist will seek to identify and describe the Religious Experience of primitive people as part of a general history and theory of man; the sociologist will concentrate on the "Social Expression" of Religious Experience, and seek to determine the nature of specifically religious groupings in relation to other groups, associations, and organizations, that constitute a given society; and the psychologist will seek to identify Religious Experience within the life of the person, and attempt to show its relation to the total structure of the self, its behavior, attitudes, and purposes, and they would all be correct in their relative focus. In all these cases, attention is directed to a Religious Experience as a phenomenon to be described as a factor that performs certain functions in human life and society. Rastafari sums this up as "Livity"; the anthropological, sociological, psychological, philosophical, and theological life and society that InI live, Think, Converse, and Exist in.

The most radical form of the denial that Religious Experience has Cognitive Import is advanced by the Logical Positivists; who hold that all assertions or forms of expression involving a term such as "God" are meaningless because there is no way in which they can be verified or falsified.

Others who hold that religious utterance based on experience is without Cognitive Import regard it either as the expression of emotions or an indication that the person using religious language has certain feelings that are associated with religion. Those who follow the lead of Ludwig Wittgenstein regard religious utterances as non-cognitive, but attempt to determine the way in which religious language is actually used within a circle of believers. Some psychologists have denied cognitive status to Religious Experience on the grounds that it represents nothing more than man's projection of his own insecurity, in the face of problems posed by life, in the world, and therefore has no referent beyond itself.

So, the question remains, as it pertains to Rastafari, are the experiences of Rastafari's Livity a religion, and its mechanisms, just religious, or can these be determined as mental projections, and/or congregational mental projections, of a sublime essence, that can be agreed upon without proof or evidence and lived daily? This is a type of complex question that only a way of life can answer. Rastafari is a "Way of Life" that embodies all the types and kinds of experiences that the religious, and others, fail to explain or agree on. Yet, to Rastafari, it all makes Heights and Overstandings. In Rastafari, Reality is individualistic and collective; sometimes without distinction.

Preface

Nascency- the condition of being Nascent: Birth, Origin. Nascent- undergoing the process of being born.

Where do we see "Religion" coming into existence in an individual? Is there a particular place, or a particular time that we can nail down as the birth or origin of "Religion"? Has religion ever sufficiently described or defined every perceptive or behavior altering reverence, of the sublime, that is carried out ritualistically?

The word Religion is defined as: Belief in and reverence for a supernatural power or powers regarded as creator and governor of the Universe; A system grounded in such belief and worship; The life or condition of a person in a religious order; A set of beliefs, values, and practices based on the teachings of a spiritual leader; A cause, a principle, or an activity pursued with zeal or conscientious devotion; To accept a higher power as a controlling influence for the good in one's life.

In Latin, it stems from the word religare, which means "to tie fast," "to tie up," or "to tie back".

Most practitioners of religion define it as the personal commitment to and serving God, or a god, with worship, devotion, and conduct, in accord with divine commands. Especially as found in accepted sacred writings or declared by authoritative teachers as a Way of Life; recognized as incumbent on true believers, and typically the relating of oneself to an organized body. This body would also evolve into institutionalized expressions of sacred beliefs, observances, and social practices, found within a given "Culture Context". A Code of Conduct would be the set of moral teachings and values that all religions have in some form. Such a code, or ethic, tells believers how to conduct their lives. It instructs them how to act towards the deity and towards one another. Religious Codes of Conduct differ in many ways, but most agree on several major themes. For example, they stress some form of the golden rule, which states that believers ideally should treat others as they would like to be treated themselves. A religion's Code of Conduct may also determine such matters as whom believers may marry, what jobs they may hold, how they dress, and what foods they may eat.

Religious Rituals include the acts and ceremonies by which believers appeal to and serve God, deities, or other sacred powers. Some rituals are performed by individuals alone, and others by groups of worshipers. Religious

Groups perform their important rituals according to a schedule and often repeat them regularly. The performance of a ritual is often called a service. Leaders of rituals often require special training and must be authorized before they are allowed to lead. This training and authorization are sometimes called ordination. There are some rituals that are led by those who are chosen because of some uniqueness. Shamans, for example, are Holy Men and Wombmen who are believed to have special powers to communicate with the gods or the spirit world. Many Shamans are thought to leave their bodies while in a trance, taking "Spirit Journeys" to find answers or healing for their people.

The most common ritual is prayer. Through prayer, a believer or someone on behalf of believers addresses concerns and thoughts to an object of worship. Prayer includes requests, expressions of thanksgiving, confessions of sins, and praise. Most major religions have a daily schedule of prayer.

Meditation, in some ways like prayer, is a Spiritual Exercise important in Asian religions. Buddhist Monks strive to be masters of meditation. By clearing the mind of day-to-day distractions, people who meditate attempt to gain a higher form of consciousness.

Many religions have rituals intended to purify the body. For example, Hindus consider the waters of the Ganges River, in India, to be sacred. Every year, millions of Hindus purify their bodies by bathing in the river, especially at the Holy City of Varanasi.

In some religions, pilgrimages are significant rituals. Pilgrimages are journeys to the sites of holy objects or to places credited with miraculous healing powers. Believers also make pilgrimages to sacred places, such as the birthplace or tomb of the founder of their faith. All devout Muslims hope to make a pilgrimage to Mecca, the birthplace of Muhammad. Many Christians travel to the Holy Land, today in the nation of Israel and a Palestinian territory called the West Bank. This land is where Yeshua (Jesus) of Nazareth lived, worked, and ministered.

Many rituals are scheduled at certain times of the day, week, or year. Various religions have services at sunrise, in the morning, at sunset, and in the evening. Special services mark the beginning of a new year. Many religions celebrate springtime, harvest time, and the new or full moon. Religious attention to the marking of the seasons may be a survival from prehistoric and ancient religions. These early religions attempted to secure the survival of the community through good harvests and hunting, which depended on a knowledge of the seasons.

XIII

Other rituals commemorate events in the history of religions. For example, the Jewish Festival of Passover recalls the meal the Israelites ate just before their departure from slavery in Egypt. Various Christian celebrations of Holy Communion are related to the last meal Yeshua (Jesus) shared with His disciples before His Elevation.

Rituals also mark important events in a person's life. Various ceremonies make such events as birth, marriage, and death into sacred occasions. Some rituals accept young people into the religion and into adult society. These rituals are called rites of passage. In Judaism, the ritual of circumcision is performed on male infants. Some Christians baptize babies soon after birth. Other Christians baptize only youths or adults.

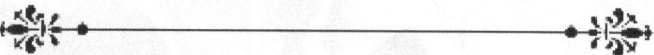

There are three main philosophical views regarding the existence of a deity: (1) Theists believe in a deity or deities. (2) Atheists believe that no deity exists. (3) Agnostics say that the existence of a deity cannot be proved or disproved. Most major religions are theistic, they teach that deities govern or greatly influence human actions as well as events in nature. Some religions are not theistic. Examples include Confucianism and some forms of Buddhism.

Religions that acknowledge only one god are called monotheistic. Judaism, Christianity, and Islam are examples of monotheistic religions. The Ancient Greeks and Romans had Polytheistic religions. Each of their many gods and goddesses had one or more special areas of influence. For example, Aphrodite was the Greek goddess of love, and Mars was the Roman god of war. In Henotheistic religions, the worship of supreme deity does not deny the existence and power of other deities. For example, Hinduism teaches that a world spirit called Brahman is the Supreme Power. But Hindus also worship numerous other gods and goddesses. Many people in Africa and the Pacific Islands also worship a Supreme Power as well as many other deities.

The followers of some Religions worship deities who are, or were people, or that are images of people. The Ancient Egyptian people considered their Pharaohs to be living gods. Before World War II (1939-1945), the Japanese honored their emperor as divine. Taoists believe in deities that look and act like human beings. They also worship some deities who were once human beings and became gods or goddesses after death.

Many people worship nature gods, these are deities who dwell in or control various aspects of nature. The Chinese, in particular, have worshiped gods of the soil and grain. Followers of Shinto worship kami, spirits that live in nature. Some American Indians worship a spirit power, a mysterious, powerful force in nature.

Among the major religions, Christianity, Hinduism, Buddhism, and Islam teach a doctrine of salvation. They stress that salvation is the highest goal of the faithful and one that all followers should try to achieve. Religions differ, however, in their understanding of salvation, when and how it occurs, and how it can be gained. In many religions, the quest for salvation is aided by the work of a "Savior." The Savior may be a god or some other divine figure, or the individual on whose teachings the religion is based.

A Doctrine of Salvation is based on the belief that individuals or groups are in some danger from which they must be "saved." The danger may be the threat of physical misfortune in this world, such as diseases or war, or the danger may await people in the life after death. Christianity and several other religions teach that the danger is primarily spiritual and is centered in each person's soul. This soul is thought to be that part of a person that survives after the body dies.

Christianity teaches that people are sinful by nature. They can, however, wipe out their sinfulness and past offenses toward God and humanity by believing in the sacrificial death of Yeshua (Jesus). If a Christian is saved, then the soul enters a state of eternal happiness, often called heaven. If a person is not saved, the soul may spend eternity in a state of punishment, often called hell.

Most Eastern religions teach that a person gains salvation by finding release from obstacles that can block human fulfillment. In most Asian religions, the obstacles take the form of worldly desires and attachments to material things. Salvation depends on whether people can free themselves from these desires and attachments, which only bring suffering.

Hinduism teaches that each person's soul, called Atman, is identical with the Supreme Spirit, Brahman, that is the source of all material creation. Hindus believe they achieve a kind of immortality, as well as union with their god, through discovering the Brahman in themselves.

In Buddhism, a person must undertake the difficult task of purification by following a set of guidelines called the Noble Eightfold Path. By following this path, people rid themselves of the delusions that doom them to an endless cycle of birth, suffering, death, and rebirth.

Islam teaches that good actions in this life brings salvation in the next. Followers must "submit" their whole selves to the will of Allah through daily prayer and other acts of worship called the Five Pillars of Islam. By following these practices, Muslims will be saved from future punishment by Allah.

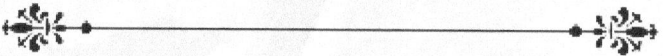

For thousands of years, followers of religions have believed in sacred stories, sometimes called myths or legends. Religious leaders often use these stories to dramatize their teachings.

Originally, people told stories to describe how the sacred powers influenced the world. The stories showed how the sacred powers directly or indirectly caused some feature or event in the world. Many stories described the creation of the world. Others told how human beings, or a particular people began. Some of the stories try to explain the causes of natural occurrences, such as thunderstorms or the changes in seasons.

Today, there are scientific explanations for many of the subjects dealt with in sacred stories. But some religious groups still insist that the stories are true in every detail. Other groups believe only in the message contained in the stories, not in the specific details. Still, other religious groups regard sacred stories as symbolic expressions of the ideals and values of their faith.

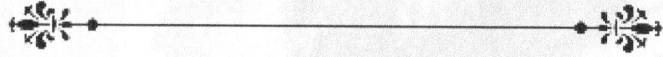

It is said that "the devil is in the details", so if that be the case, let's discover the details, and why the devil is inlay, waiting.

What do we think about Religion? What would We say is Religion, and what would We say is not Religion? More importantly, why would We declare something positive or negative to the realm in which Religion supposedly affects? That injury is exactly what We are doing when We speak to the affirmation or denial of what is or is not Religion.

As a concept, Religion has undergone considerable debate throughout times. How to define Religion obviously affects the scope of the study of Religion, and what it means. The comparative study of Religion has posed problems for Traditional Western Ideas, because the West has typically thought of Religion as involving a set of beliefs, values, practices, and beliefs in, and responses to God, or the gods, based on the teachings of a spiritual leader. For some Eastern Religions, God, or the gods, is not important, and there may be no Creator God - the emphasis rather is upon liberation from this World and its influences.

XVI

Another question concerns whether Religion is simply to be regarded as a human phenomenon and human construction, or whether it has some kind of transcendent origin and reference-point.

No simple definition can describe the many Religions in the World. Every society has a Religion. For many people, Religion is an organization & system of beliefs, rituals (acts and ceremonies), personal practices, and worship directed towards a supreme power or deity, or god. For others, Religion involves a number of gods or deities. Some people follow Religions that worship no specific god or gods. There are also people who practice their own Religious beliefs in a personal way, largely independent of any organized Religion.

Almost all people who participate in a Religion believe that a Divine Power is at Work in the World. Some believe that this Power Created the World and can influence their lives in various ways. Others believe that the goal of Human Life is to live in Harmony with this Power.

In its most basic sense, Religion deals with the primary concerns of: What is the purpose of life? What is the final destiny of human beings and animals? What is the difference between right and wrong? What is the meaning of suffering and evil? And what are a person's obligations to other people and to the World?

People practice Religions for many reasons. Some anthropologists believe that the Religious Impulse may be one of the most fundamental traits of the human species. Throughout the World, many people follow a Religious Tradition simply because it is a part of the heritage of their nation, culture, tribe, ethnic group or family. One objective of Religion is to give groups a sense of identity and purpose.

Religion can provide a sense of personal security in a confusing World, because believers feel that a supreme power, God, watches over them. Believers may request help or protection from their god or gods through prayer or ritual.

Many people follow a Religion because it promises them happiness in life or in some kind of life after death, or they believe it will save them from eternal damnation. The prospect of an afterlife also offers hope to those who suffer in this life. Religion provides individual fulfillment in this way and helps people to understand their place in the universe.

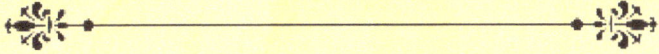

XVII

There are thousands of Religions in the World. The eight major ones are Buddhism, Christianity, Confucianism, Hinduism, Islam, Judaism, Shinto, and Taoism. Hinduism, Shinto, and Taoism developed over many centuries. The other five Religions base their faith on the life or teachings of specific men. They are, (I) for Buddhism, Siddhartha Gautama, whom became known as Gautama Buddha; (2) for Confucianism, Confucius; and (3) for Judaism, Christianity, and Islam, Abraham and Moses, Yeshua (Jesus), and Muhammad.

The Religion that traces their history to individuals follow a general pattern of development. During the individual's lifetime, or soon after his death, a distinctive system of worship and ceremonies develop; based on the individual's life and teachings. In addition to inspiring worship, the individual represented an ideal way of life that followers try to imitate.

The Teachings of Religions have shaped the lives of people since prehistoric times. Judaism, Islam, and especially Christianity, have been major influences in the formation of Western culture. These Religions are called Religions of the Book because they all are at least partly inspired by the Hebrew Bible or Old Testament. These three faiths, particularly Islam, have also played a crucial role in the latter development of Middle Eastern and African culture. The cultures of Asia have been shaped by Buddhism, Confucianism, Hinduism, Shinto, and Taoism.

Experts think prehistoric Religions arose out of fear and wonder about natural events, such as storms, earthquakes, and the birth of babies. To explain why someone died, people credited supernatural powers greater than themselves or greater than the World around them.

Prehistoric people most likely centered their Religious activities on the most important elements of their existence, such as adequate rainfall or success in hunting. They often placed food, ornaments, and tools in the graves of members of the group who had died. They probably believed that these items would be useful to, or desired by, the dead. Archaeologists believe that prehistoric people drew pictures and may have performed other rituals intended to promote the fertility of women and animals and to ensure good hunting. They likely made sacrifices for the same reason.

The organization of the World's major Religions ranges from simple to complex. Many Religions have spiritual leaders, often called the clergy. These leaders have the authority and responsibility to conduct Religious services, to advise or command believers, and to govern the Religious organization at various levels. In some Religions the laity, that is the believers who are not members of the clergy, also have important roles.

XVIII

In many countries, there is a state (official or favored) Religion. For example, Islam is the state Religion of Iran, Pakistan, Saudi Arabia, and many other nations. Lutheranism is the state Religion of Denmark and Norway, and Buddhism is the state Religion of the Asian nations of Bhutan, Cambodia, and Thailand. The United Kingdom has two established (official) churches, the Church of England, which is Anglican, and the Church of Scotland which is Presbyterian.

Judaism has no one person as its head. Each local congregation of synagogues supervise its own affairs, usually under the leadership of a rabbi. Israel and a few other countries have chief rabbis. These rabbis are scholars who serve as the top judges of Religious law.

Christian denominations (groups) are organized in various ways. In the Roman Catholic Church, believers are organized in various districts called parishes, which belong to larger districts called dioceses. Dioceses, in turn, belong to provinces. The main diocese in each province is called an archdiocese. Pastors preside over parishes, bishops over dioceses, and archbishops over archdioceses. The Pope presides over the entire Roman Catholic Church with the advice and assistance of high officials called cardinals. Some Protestant denominations are governed by similar patterns of hierarchies (levels of authority). Others are governed by boards of the clergy and laity or by local congregations. Throughout most history, women have had fewer rights and a lower social status than men. Largely because of women's lower status, most Religious hierarchies have tended to exclude women from leadership roles.

Confucianism and Islam have no ordained clergy. Leadership is provided by scholars who interpret Religious teachings. In Shinto and Taoism, the basic organizational unit is the priesthood. In Buddhism, the chief unit is an order of monks called the Sangha. The monks serve as advisers and teachers and play a vital part in everyday life. In some Buddhist countries, the head of state is also the leader of the national order of monks.

Hinduism has no consistent pattern of hierarchy or organization. There are no congregations or parishes. Hindus tend to worship individually or in families. Services in temples are performed by the Brahmans, members of the highest Hindu caste (social class).

What has just been conveyed is only a minute synopsis of structure as it pertains to religions. There are many different, similar, misunderstood, strict, liberal, formal, informal, international, indigenous, public, secretive, authoritative, and democratic religions. There seems to be almost one religion for every mindset that exist; that includes the formally enslaved physically, but later mentally enslaved people. Rastafari deflects, deviates, and diverges, but is actually worthier of being held in the same, if not higher, regard as any religion in and of this world. If not, then where can a position be taken, other than Rastafari, that would produce a balanced, centered, perspective that would possibly render answers to some of the most puzzling questions Iniversally known to Us?

    Religion is like the clouds in Our atmosphere. Depending on the latitude and longitude, the season, and the temperature, those clouds can produce thunderstorms, snow storms, hail storms, and even extreme humidity, that makes temperatures hotter; even without extra sunlight. But on certain occasions, those same clouds create beautiful scenic pleasures like blended shape aesthetics, merging color aesthetics, and feelings of serene intuitive agape.

    So, how can We be autodidactive in Religion and gain the discernment of effects and effectiveness in order to understand what would allow a balanced, centered erudition? In religion, as hard as some may try, you can't. Only a Way of Life can produce an autodidactive, discerning, balanced erudition of creation and its Knowledge, Wisdom, and Overstanding. Rastafari is InI way of life. Rastafari defines religion and so much more.

Introduction

By the rivers of Babylon, there we sat down, yea, we wept, when we remembered Zion… For there they that carried us away captive required of us a song; and they that wasted us required of us mirth, saying, sing us one of the songs of Zion. How shall we sing the Lord's song in a strange land?

A physical, religious, social, ideological oppression is what sparks the emergence of a Rastafari. It is the trumpet blowing and the drums beating. It is the solemnity of the spirit announcing the solemn chants. It is what provokes the search for Truth, the Emotions of Righteousness, and the Courage of Law.

Rastafari seems to be Afro-centric from the observable outset, but it is more than just that. It is Afro-centric when InI are in discussions and explaining to man his self. It is Afro-centric when InI are describing societies & civilizations and their origins. And, it is Afro-centric when education, science, and even medicine are the subjects and topics. But it elevates and grows into…

Rastafari is Abrahamic; in that, it has one "Mono" God at its core. Rastafari hears, in his mind's heart, Jah, when he says, "Get thee out of thy country, and from thy kindred, and from thy father's house, unto a land that I will show thee" … and … "Babylon the great is fallen, is fallen, and is become the habitation of devils, and the hold of every foul spirit, and a cage of every unclean and hateful bird. For all nations have drunk of the wine of the wrath of her fornication, and the Kings of the earth have committed fornication with her… Come out of her, my people, that ye be not partakers of her sins, and that ye receive not of her plagues"!!

As Rastafari reasons, within I self, a grounding will create the foundation of I journey through the Spiritual Mystical Heights of Life Livity. The Mind's Eye will search, The Mind's Heart will find, and the Mind's Expression will manifest into Rastafari. This is the unique, ambiguous, ameliorating, and procreation of Jah's Light in InI inimitably.

Part of Rastafari's identity is with him being "sententious". It is a most efficient way in giving the teachings to those uninitiated. Rastafari can also be a practitioner of solecism, which allows patios and jargon to be used efficaciously.

XXI

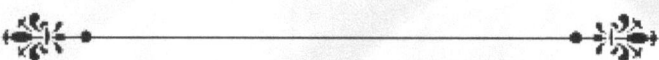

We begin with the supernal and empyrean Ethiopia. An ideal, belief, culture, identity, society, and nation. This Ethiopia has a history that stretches back before there was a time, and a future that goes on in the same way.

Ethiopia first comes to InI, contemporarily, Biblically. In the book of Genesis, taught as one of the first books of Moses, in chapter two, verse thirteen, it tells of a second river named Gihon, and that it is the same as that one that "compasseth the whole land of Ethiopia". This early reference in the Holy Bible, as part of the summary of creation, is a powerful mention. It gives great truth, grants worthiness, and conducts reverence towards Ethiopia.

The Bible speaks of Ethiopia no fewer than twenty (20) times, Ethiopian no fewer than eight (8) times, and Ethiopians no fewer than thirteen (13) times. Cush, Ethiopia's Biblical a.k.a, is spoken of another eight (8) times. Also, Ethiopia is historically referred to and called Abyssinia.

Authentic Rastafari history nascents from the Bible in the verses concerning King Solomon and the Queen of Sheba, Makeda (1 Kings 10:1-13; 2 Chronicles 9: 1-12). This monograph gives an account of a "nota bene" of ancient history, but not of the hagiography of Queen Empress Makeda, and her magnificent elevation, emulation, and condition of eminence received from King Solomon; and initiated in and with her people. We do not get a codex of the two rulers, but a precis, being one-sided, concerned with the patriarchy of King Solomon, instead of the harmonics of spirituality that both rulers, both genders, both ideals, held.

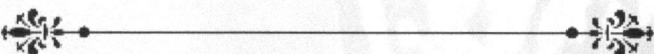

InI need to be clear, before going any further, that in 1928 and 1930 (the 20th century), 2000 years in the waiting of prophecy to be fulfilled, as was expected, Jah, in His creative image and likeness, was crowned. No one else fits the Biblical Criteria other than H.I.M. Haile Selassie 1st of Ethiopia.

No one in the measurement or parameters of the messianic principles had or has, the qualifications and certifications of H.I.M., and this is an absolute fact.

While all authority, Kingship, Queenship, and the like, are given from JAH, only Ethiopia has had the privilege to maintain a King of Kings and Lord of Lords on the throne. This is clearly a Divine Right. And to maintain that, with being of the Tribe of Judah, and having the scepter remaining in the divinely, ordained, anointed, hands of the Solomonic Line of Kings of Ethiopia, InI can now claim the reward of this Knowledge, Wisdom, and Overstanding.

No one or nation can steal from JAH! No one or nation can take by force that which JAH has given to or granted another. So, when InI read that "Ethiopia Shall soon stretch out her hands unto God"; "The Sceptre Shall not Depart from Judah nor a Lawgiver from between His Feet"; and "Thine house and thy Kingdom shall be established for-Iver before thee: Thy Throne shall be established for-Iver," InI should look for these things to exist. InI should know that these things are Truth.

Jah does not, and is not capable, of lying, His Truth extends For-Iver! JAH is the God of gods, and a Lord of Kings, and a revealer of secrets. This is why most find it difficult to know. They do not place themselves in the position, status, or state to know Truth.

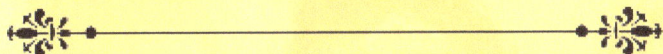

Blessed is the man that endureth temptation; for when he is tried, he shall receive the crown of life, which JAH has promised to them that love H.I.M. Rastafari is the only Oneness with a Crown. The Root of David has prevailed to open the Book and to loose the Seven Seals thereof. InI revel in these Seven Seals daily, through InI chakras. Rastafari anticipates the Overstanding gained in knowing the completion of I Self in them.

..." And on His head, were many crowns...", His Imperial Majesty was crowned King in 1928, receiving one crown, and Emperor, King of Kings, in 1930, receiving another that is a "Triple Crown", this is how InI know this aspect of Prophecy. "He had a name written, that no man knew but Himself", JAH Ras Tafari is and was and will be H.I.M. A name that was elevated to Haile Selassie I upon becoming King of Kings, Lord of Lords. An ancient ritual that belongs solely to Ethiopia's Divinity. Haile Selassie means "Power of The Trinity", this Trinity is the "Word of God". This is the inspiration that inspired the Prophets to write about it.

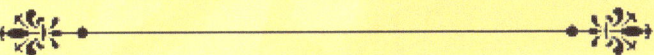

The Holy scriptures are allegorical in some places, figurative in some, and literal in others, and there is an expected degree of misunderstandings from the neophyte. But after study, when the allegorical, figurative, and literal all speak about the same Man, doing the same thing, being the same way, then that becomes "Absolute Truth".

"And out of His mouth goeth a sharp sword, that with it, He should smite the nations; and He shall rule them with a rod of Iron..." His Imperial Majesty is the only leader that has addressed the League of Nations and the United Nations, two bodies of the collectiveness of the world's nations, The League of Nations, the predecessor of the United Nations, is where He described exactly how nations would treat nations. And from His mouth spoke on how the death toll would be filled with the remnant left from the "casting alive into the lake of fire", those that received the mark of the beast.

"And I saw no temple therein; for the Lord God Almighty and the lamb are the temple of it". This is where it gets personal. JAH and the Lamb are the temple, and the temple is within. Therefore, InI must be in the same image and likeness of JAH. This is not to bring JAH down. This is an identifying factor to know that InI can and must Elevate.

His Imperial Majesty is Christ in His Kingly character. But just like there wasn't many people believing the previous time this has happened, there won't be a majority knowing this time either. Similar things run parallel in this Iniverse. That is why it is so important to know InI Majesty in order to prevent the destruction that InI people are placing on each other.

Rastafari in "I"

Ezeki-El 44:15-30; InI are a Tribe of Priests unknown and unrecognized to the world because InI belong to The Most High JAH RASTAFARI. InI are completely His, coming near, standing before, entering in, and keeping the charge of JAH! InI shall have Locks, shall Teach InI people the difference between the Holy and Profane, and cause them to discern between the unclean and the clean. InI shall Judge in controversy, according to His Judgement, Laws, and statues in assemblies; and Hallow His Sabbaths, not man's Sabbath's, JAH's Sabbaths.

- Psalms 68:4; Sing, Extol, and Rejoice is to find Peace in the Negation of negativity in One's life. It is to combat negativity with positivity. Positive Vibrations, Higher Vibrations, Life and Living Vibrations.
- John 4:23, In the Spirit will all things Truly take place; Spiritual, Mystical, Empyreal, Celestial, Elevated, Sublime, Enlightened, Majestic, Noble, High Consciously, Morally and Intellectually Worthy.
- Luke 17: 20-21; It is No-Thing to just see with the Physical, Natural Eye, Externally. Since the Kingdom is within, the Discovery of it must come from a Beckoning, Urgency, Meditation, Contemplation, or Revelation.

XXIV

- Roman 8:14; When InI perceive InI Divine Self, know that InI are Indeed Divine beings. InI look for the Assistance of The Most High JAH RASTAFARI. This Assistance develops InI Overstanding of JAH's Statues, Laws, and Covenants; therefore, InI begin to "Be Led" by The Spirit of JAH and become the sons of JAH.
- Romans 14:5; Here is where InI confirm that InI are indeed Creators of InI Reality. InI set criteria, standards, and construct conditions that InI begin to Live by. This is the Full Persuasion that InI affect with potency in I Life.
- 1 Corinthians 3:16; There comes a point when InI must know, Period, Point Blank, Absolutely! Am I Divine or Am I not? Knowing this is the quintessential mandate of Rastafari! It must be a conviction of Mind, Heart, and Spirit, carried out in InI actions.
- 2 Corinthians 6:16; The Temple of JAH is a Singularity! No-Thing can exist with it. It does not compromise. When JAH says "I will dwell in them, ...walk In them..., ...Be their JAH..., Be I people, all of them that adheres to being That Temple, that singularity becomes JAH.
- 1 Timothy 6:15-16; The feeling is Completeness, Truth, Renewed Heights, Absolute Love, Direction, Coalescing, Vision. At this point, InI must be a Natural Leader Being: Self-Confident, Knowledgeable of mankind, Maker of Own decisions, Ambitious, Original in Own methods, Joyous in Commanding others, Motivated by Personal Interest, and Independent; while also being the Spiritual Leader: Having Confidence in JAH, Knowing JAH, Seeks JAH's Will in InI will, Being Self-Effacing, Following JAH's Methods, Enjoying serving all, being motivated by love, and JAH dependent.

"Rise oh JAH, and Let Thine Enemies Be Scattered, and Let Them That Hate Thee Flee Before Thee!

 *Rastafari Livity*

Chapter One

Word, Sound, Power

    The adoration of His Imperial Majesty, Haile Selassie 1ˢᵗ, in the Way of Life of Rastafari, is the earliest and most natural forms of Heights Expression. The complex modern theologies of the Rastafari Man and Wombman are merely the involvements and amplifications of this simple and Aboriginal Vibration. Rastafari's Mind, recognizing the Beneficent Power of Image and Likeness with H.I.M., adores Emperor Haile Selassie 1ˢᵗ as the Manifestation of the Supreme Creator of the Iniverse.

    Jah Rastafari, Haile Selassie 1ˢᵗ, is the Spark and Innate Fire of InI body, the Fire of Nature. His Imperial Majesty is the Author of Life, the Thunder of Creation, and nascention of all. Without H.I.M. there is no movement, no existence, no form. Jah Rastafari is immense, indivisible, imperishable, and everywhere present. It is InI's need of His Light and Creative Energy that is felt by all Rastafari Man, Wombman, and Child; and nothing is more fearful to Rastafari than His non-revelation.

    H.I.M.'s Beneficent Influences cause InI to correlate His identification with the Principle of Good, H.I.M. is the Personification of Truth, the regenerating Principle of Righteousness, and the Fecundity of Rightness, which perpetuates and rejuvenates this world's undeserving existence.

Rastafari Livity

Rastafari knows that the Power and Light of His Imperial Majesty, Haile Selassie 1st, of Ethiopia, has always been worshiped by man in his many religious ways. Among all the nations of antiquity, altars, mounds, and temples were dedicated to the worship of His Reflective Power and Light. The ruins of these consecrated and sacred places remain with InI, in some capacity. Notable among them being the Great Pyramids of Kemet, the mounds of the American Indigenous, the Zikkurats of Babylon and Chaldea, the Round Towers of Ireland, and even the massive rings of uncut stones in Britain and Normandy. The early priests, sages, and prophets, of these sacred rites, were versed in the Essential Nature of His Imperial Majesty's Power and Light, and not just in the outward appearance of its many manifestations, or the limitations of their environment and resources. Their writings are best Overstood when read and studied in light of this ideal.

With the growth of man's knowledge of the constitution and periodicity of the heavenly bodies, astronomical principles and terminologies were introduced into his understanding of H.I.M.'s Power and Light. A division and hierarchy was established, giving tutelary gods planetary thrones and celestial bodies the names of multiple deities. The stars were divided into constellations, and these were further named for all of the attributes of H.I.M.'s Power and Light. History and anthropology have revealed that this proclivity is a universal development of many cultures of antiquity.

The Visible Supreme, among the people of antiquity, was assigned to the highest of the gods, and became symbolic of the Supreme Authority of the Creator Himself. From a deep philosophic consideration of the powers and principles of H.I.M.'s origin has come the concept of the Trinity; as it is understood by the world today. The tenet of a Triune Divinity is not peculiar to Christian or Mosaic theology, but forms a conspicuous part of the dogma of the greatest religions of both ancient and modern times. The Persians, Hindus, Babylonians, and Egyptians, had their Trinities. In every instance, these represented the threefold (creative, destructive, rebirth) form of one Supreme Intelligence. Rastafari knows this Trinity as One Love, One Aim, One Destiny; for the name, Haile Selassie, means in Amharic, Power of the Trinity.

The tenet of the Trinity became a science when the knowledge of Time was realized. The day, with its morning, noon, and night, gave rise to what the Trinity essentially is. Sages and philosophers therefore divided the life of all things into three distinct parts: growth, maturity, and decay.

Rastafari Livity

The Circadian of Jah's Resplendent Glory is revealed in the magnificent sky displays every dawn, noon, and evening. Jah, Pro-Creator of the world, is symbolized by the dawn. His Royal Purple and Blue is clearly seen at this time of rising. Jah The Begotten, the Illuminating One, sent to bear witness before all the worlds, is the celestial noon day, radiant and magnificent; the maned Lion of Judah, Savior of the World. His Golden Color represents His Power without end. Jah's Spirit is the evening, robed in flaming red, allowing that which has dwelled in darkness to know of His Light. It seems to vanish into darkness, but it is actually roaming in the lower worlds, announcing an impending resurrection of His Power and Light; rising triumphantly, again, from the embrace of darkness.

Rastafari nascents from the Black Nationalist Pan-African Ideal of the early 1900s. It evolved into an identity that was specific to Ethiopia; because of the purity of her never being colonized. The Emperor, Haile Selassie 1 (the first) is the procatarctic of InI Royal Identity with Jah, initiating an interpreted reflection of modern prophet and priesthood; with Hebraic and Ethiopian Orthodox Christianity, and Islamic elements.

Rastafari believes in Jah of Abraham, the One Jah Almighty, maker of all that can be, both visible and invisible: and in the messianic traditions of a savior and redeemer, homoiousian with Jah Almighty, being His Imperial Majesty, Haile Selassie 1 of Ethiopia. Born from the lineage of King Solomon of Israel and Queen Makeda (Queen of Sheba) of Ethiopia, Monophysite as of His Nature, Hypostasis in Identity. Revealed in the Divine Words of Jah, in His Holy Scripture, in Psalms 2,8,16,22,24,40,41,45,68,69,72,89,101,102,110,118; in 1st Timothy 6:15, and in Revelation 5,11,14, and 19 as Overstood in InI Heights.

For InI, His Imperial Majesty came down from the Heights of the Heavens, by the Power of the Holy Spirit. He became flesh for InI in order to reconcile InI to H.I.M. The Father is revealed to InI in His Kingly Character as Savior of the World. He is revealed to redeem His Lost Hearts and Spiritual Minds. InI was spiritually sick, and InI nature began to tremble; with a demand to be healed; fallen, needing to be raised up; dead, waiting to Live again. Enslaved, InI had lost the possession of the good; it was necessary for it to be given back to InI. Closed in the darkness of the Western Hemisphere, it was necessary to bring InI the Light. Captives of Greco-Roman Eurocentric Ideals, InI suffered and waited for InI

Rastafari Livity

Savior. Prisoners needing help, still being treated as slaves, InI required a liberator. Are these things minor or insignificant? Did they not move Jah once or twice before, and now, to descend His Spirit into human form and nature, and visit InI, since humanity is in so miserable a state?

The spirit, became flesh in order to be InI model of Holy Righteousness. To make InI partakers of the Divine Nature. This is why the Spirit became Man, and the Spirit of Jah became the Son of Man, again. So that man, by entering into communion with the Spirit, and the spirit within, may receive Divine Sonship, and become the Sons of Jah. Having InI sharing in His Divinity, assuming InI nature, so that H.I.M. might make man into gods.

At all times and in every race, anyone who fears Jah and does what is righteous and true has been made acceptable to H.I.M. He has, however, Willed to make men holy and redeem them, not as individuals without any bond or link between them, but, rather to make them into a priesthood who might acknowledge H.I.M. and serve H.I.M. in Holiness. To live with this Wisdom is Rastafari's only requirement. For what man knoweth the things of a man, save the spirit of man which is in H.I.M.? Even so, the things of Jah knoweth no man, but the Spirit of Jah. Now InI have received, not the spirit of the world, but the Spirit which is of Jah; that InI might know the things that are freely given to InI of Jah as Spiritual Duty. This is the mystery. This is the Heights. This is the Oneness.

The People of Jah are marked by characteristics that clearly distinguish them from all other religious, ethnic, political, or cultural groups, found in history. God is not the property of any one people. But as Jah, He acquired a people for Himself from those who previously were not even considered people; made into a "chosen people, chosen race, a royal priesthood, and a holy nation". One becomes a member of this people not by physical birth, but by being born spiritually, and then even mystically. Jah's People have for "Their Head" His Imperial Majesty, Haile Selassie 1st, of Ethiopia, the anointed King of Kings, Lord of Lords, Conquering Lion of the Tribe of Judah. And because of this same anointing, the Holy Spirit flows from the Head into the body, this is the "Messianic People" of this millennium. The status of this people is wholly that of the dignity and liberty of the Sons of Jah, in whose hearts the Holy Spirit dwells as the "New Ark of The Covenant".

Rastafari Livity

No census is, or can be made, attributed to Rastafari's population, because all men/women are called to belong to the "New Family of Jah" in Spirit. This Family, therefore, while remaining one and only one, is to be spread, and found, throughout the whole world, and to all ages, in order that the design of Jah's Will be fulfilled. For Jah created, formed, and then made humans "Beings" and human nature One, and One it shall be. If there seems to be any deviation to this, then those deviators will find themselves outside the "Walls" and in the "Abyss", shuffling through "Darkness", recipient of the "Curses" and reciprocal of their own wicked, unrighteous machinations.

With so much of today's religious and spiritual information and knowledge available to InI, how is it that most people are still lost when it comes to the subject of Spirit, and specifically Rastafari? How is it that Spiritual Blindness is the dominant trait perceived, in the doubter, by those who search a little, and seek a little more? InI live in an information age, but some do not want knowledge, or information, if it is going to make them accountable, or responsible, and that is just for the perceivable, observable manifestations. What about the hidden, non-tangible, and beyond manifestations? InI have to discover the depth and breadth of the inner system and ability of Rastafari that allows InI to see all things, all states, and all conditions, for the betterment of InI Self and those chosen to see.

Rastafari, a quest for the hidden truth and wisdom, is an inner system, innate ability, and Way of Life, that assists the neoteric, combative, striving energy in InI and around InI; which has become common place now in InI society by those searching for truth and equipollence.

Religion has become exfoliate, and in its exfoliation, it is further exfoliated as the gap of division becomes more concretized. Rastafari is an ancient ability that can remove the "Fission Effect", and crippling, that the Exfoliation in Religion is causing. Rastafari has undergone a cosmetic surgery to its meaning, in InI times, in order to make it either more appealing or repulsive,

Rastafari Livity

depending on whose exegesis is entertained. But let InI now actuate a revelation, that can give InI true meaning towards applicability. That will cease any foolish thinking and acceptance of the philosophy of categorization, denomination, sect, tribe, or any individual's grouping; fueling a divisional and separatist subconscious ideology.

Rastafari is a Gnostic, Hermeneutic, Neoteric Spiritual Experience, that emphasizes the Immediate Awareness of Jah. It is an expression of the innate tendency of human beings towards complete harmony with Jah.

Mystical elements are found in all religions, although a stronger reference is now acknowledged in Rastafari. In Rastafari exist major elements, even in the historical, of the greatest character and attributes of holy men. His Imperial Majesty, Haile Selassie the First, of Ethiopia teaches InI that, "all of the mystics agree, speak the same language, and dwell in the same ideal realm". Therefore, it is incumbent of Rastafari to think, speak, and have in appearance, the personality, character, and identity of a sage, maven, priest, and/or prophet.

Rastafari can sometimes be called an interior life, because its Mystical Way does involve withdrawal from, and the renunciation of, the manifest world, its conditions, and states of being.

The Heights of Rastafari is "union with the divine and sacred". Ras Tafari, Head Creator, is a path to that Union that is usually developed by obtaining and attaining awakening, purgation, illumination and elevation, through a conscious awareness.

Awakening- This experience is similar to conversion in its most intense form, it's comparable to sanctification. It is preceded by restlessness and uncertainty of what is already known, and there is an urge to commit to seeking a Unitive Life, and Loving Jah with one's whole being.

Purgation- This is a purification of the self and may run concurrently with later stages. It may contain several phases, such as, contrite and repentance; detachment, austerity, chastity; Extreme obedience to scripture or law; and dying to one's self. While this period may include many ascetic practices and rituals, of monastics, Rastafari is not to be confused or identified with monastics, for whom such practices are the end goal. For Rastas, they are only means and ceases after a definite period.

Rastafari Livity

Illumination- This refers to those pleasurable and exalted states in which the Rasta glimpses the Heights, and has moments of contact with Jah's Essence, even though selfhood remains. This is the level in which some people may have psychic experiences. Symbolically, it is often referred to as the prophet, messenger, priest levels. It includes a joyous apprehension of the Absolute of Jah, a heightened perception of the world, and sometimes extra sensory in touch, smell, taste, sounds, and feelings.

Union- a oneness, joining, or formation into singleness. This is when a Rasta has reached the state of direct and continuous experience, intuition, instinct, and insight with Jah and H. I.M.'s creation. A Rasta's interactions with people, at this time, may seem strange, dreamy, combative, and even wrong. There may seem to be a dualistic identity, maintaining a distinction between the Rasta and the divine, or there may be a non-dualistic identity, where no distinction is made between the divine and the Self. The true purpose of Rastafari in this way can be somewhat of a doctrine, even though Rastafari has no single or central doctrine.

Rastafari seeks to re-establish the harmony, which originally permeated Man and belonged between man and his divinized state, before the separation took place, which disturbed InI Equilibrium and Edenic state.

Rastafari's apparent denial, or self-negating, is part of a psychological process and eluding strategy that does not really deny the person. The person is there, but only in the capacity of a "Remembrance Token" for continued striving. Despite naysayers, and only with the merits of his own efforts, the more mature teachings and levels of Rastafari come in and satisfy the claims of rationality, elevation, and righteousness, for those critics. Before this, a Rastafari may seem irrational, combative, dissociative, and/or law breaking.

There is obviously something non-mental, but logical, paradoxical, and unpredictable about Rastafari, but it is not, therefore, irrational, or antirational, or religious without thought. Rather, it is a knowledge of the most adequate type and kind, only it cannot be fully expressed in words. If there is a "mystery" about the "Rastafari Experience" it is the Livity it shares with Life and the Focal Conscious Awareness of a Mystic.

 *Rastafari Livity*

Rastafari, a form, and way of living in Quantum Theory, indicates that man, a meeting place and point of various levels of reality, is more than a one-dimensional observer of three. He is a Multi-Dimensional participant of this and many other Multi-Dimensional worlds; seeing, knowing, and sometimes only glimpsing past, present, or future actions and events. Despite the interactions and correspondences between levels, surely "what's below is like what's above, they are not to be equated, but are seen as reflective and expansive. Mentally a praxis (technique) and gnosis (esoteric knowledge), Rastafari consists of a way, system, and methodology in becoming an Iniversal Transcendent Mystic Man.

The relationship of the religion of faith to Rastafari (personal religion raised to the highest power) is ambiguous, a mixture of respect and misgivings. Though Rastafari may be associated with religion, it need not be. The Rasta often represents a type that the religious institutions and organizations does not and cannot produce, and does not know what to do with if and when a Rasta appears. Although the inner core of Rastafari may be somewhat defined by mysticism, and is relatable to the origins of most religions and their founders, it is frequently considered to be a disturbing element by Judaism, Christianity, and Islam.

The founders of Rastafari may have been incipient or advanced mystics; and the inner compulsions of their experiences have proved less amenable to dogmas, creeds, and institutional restrictions, which are bound to be outward and majority oriented. There are religions of authority and the religion of spirit. Thus, there is a paradox: if the Rasta minority is distrusted or maltreated, religious life loses its sap; on the other hand, these "peculiar people" do not easily fit into society, with the requirements of a prescriptive community composed of less sensitive seekers of safety and religious routine. And though no deeply religious person can be without a touch of the mystic, that is in Rastafari, and no Rasta can be, in the deepest sense, other than, at least at one time, religious, the dialogue between Rastafari and the conventional religionist, "when it has happened, has been far from either cordial or corrigible. From both sides, there is a constant need for restatement and re-evaluation. A greater tolerance by the religionists would allow a cohesion of liberated men's worship. Though it validates religion, Rastafari also tends to escape the fetters of organized religion.

Rastafari Livity

Rastafari shares a common world with oneiromancy, theurgy (power of persuading the supernatural) prayer, worship, religion, metaphysics (transcendent levels of reality), and even science (physics, astronomy, astrology, biology, etc.). At times, it may not always be easy to distinguish Rastafari from these, but its approach and emphasis are different. Though there is an element of oneiromancy, psychism, and the occult in much of what can pass for Rastafari, it is not to be equated with a science of the unseen or with voices and visions. Powers of the occult are viewed as real, but they can also be dangerous and are not of primary interest to an elevated Rasta, who warns against their likely misuse.

Prayer and worship may form part of Rastafari's Livity, but they are viewed as means and not as essence; also, they are usually continuations of sensory experiences. Rastafari is a Pure Initary Consciousness or a Union with JAH.

Rastafari incorporates science and has always seen science as contributing to the Knowledge, Wisdom, and Overstanding, of InI Heights. It is analytic and discursive, and expresses its finding in precise and abstract formulas, which are useful in their own particular times. This is the Element of Evolution that in Rastafari is a building on Ancient Knowledge and Wisdoms, connecting them in several ways; locating the applicable range that overlaps the former and latter aspects and levels. There is always this unique coalescing paradigm that Rastafari reveals.

To define is to limit; so, therefore, no single definition will cover every aspect of Rastafari. Some have objected to any definition, and believe that Rastafari is "enlightened" or "illumination"; which themselves are vast, obscured, vague, and ambiguous Words and Concepts. Though they meet, Rastafari has to be distinguished from prophetic religions as well as from shamanism (a belief system built around psychic transformations), because even as Priest/Prophet equality among bredrens stays the same. Rastafari does its Working through chosen individuals, not necessarily saints and chosen for no other reason than JAH's Will. Rastafari emphasizes action to a far greater extent than most forms of prophetic religions, with a penchant for inwardness and the beyond.

Rastafari, in duty, is the Pursuit of Communion with, identity with, and Conscious Awareness of InI Ultimate Reality, divinity, spiritual truth, and JAH;

Rastafari Livity

through direct experience, intuition, instinct, and insight. The Rasta usually centers on practices intended to nurture those experiences. A Rasta may be dualistic, maintaining a distinction between the Self and Jah, or may be nondualistic; such pursuit has long been an integral part of the religious life of all humanity. Rastafari is a "Way of Life" and a Direct Consciousness of the Presence of JAH, the Essence of Being, in InI Livity.

Rastafari has esoteric teachings meant to explain the relationship between an unchanging, eternal, mystical, non-ending, manifestable entity and of the mortal and finite Universe, JAH's Creation. Those esoteric teachings are a science whose objective is the reparation of the heart and turning it away from all else but JAH. JAH must be seen with the inward eye and/or heart. The Height of Being One with JAH is chiefly attained in the continual remembrance of JAH through the extolling of His name as InI identity.

As InI continue on InI reparation journey, a Perennial Philosophy will become the ideal of the Rastafari's Livity. The Perennial Philosophy, also called Perennialism, is a perspective, within the philosophy of religion, which views each of the world's religious traditions as sharing a single, Iniversal Truth; on which the foundations of all religious knowledge and doctrine has grown. According to the Perennial Philosophy, the mystical experiences in all religions are essentially the same. It supposes that many, if not all of the world's great religions, have risen around the teaching of mystics. Including Abraham, Moses, Yeshua, Muhammad, Buddha, Loatze, etc.... It also sees most religious traditions as describing the fundamental mystical experience, at least esoterically.

This idea is given merit through The "Common Core-Thesis". The Common Core-Thesis says that different descriptions can mask quite similar, if not identical, experiences. It makes it clear that people can differentiate experience from interpretation, such that different interpretations may be applied to otherwise identical experiences. Rastafari is taught, through H.I.M., that "all the mystics agree" which is described through Perennial Philosophy and Common Core-Thesis as definitive reasons Rastafari can apply this perspective logically.

Rastafari Livity

    Some confusion can come from the application of a mystic's teachings, or way of life, outside of his or her traditional ways. The determinant does not want to lose, release, or share their particular archetype's teachings; feeling robbed of some essential aspect of it. This is the thing described as religion by Rastafari. That binding, tying, concretizing, the philosophies of an Enlightened Being is a horrific injury to the world, in Rastafari's Heights. Why would any lover of truth not want that truth to be spread to its greatest applicable reach? Why would any lover of life not want their contribution to life emitted to the world from their source of life? Rastafari knows this, and cordially educate itself of his Brethren's Elevation.

    Rastafari is concerned with one thing and one thing only, and that is for the betterment of "All People". InI want Homo Sapiens to Rise and Stand Spiritually Tall. Rastafari wants Man to be Strong and True. InI want for Jah to Permeate and Coalesce in InI Reality, Manifestly. Rastafari knows that this want is a necessary and fundamental truth; a law of the divine and absolute, secular and finite. One "Athenaeum" should be made available to all people, so that a complete and higher learning can take place. In this way, ever increasing "Heights" would remove the suffering of ignorance. The interactions between the "so called" races would become more peaceful and productive, instead of hostile, volatile, conflicts that are being currently engaged in.

Rastafari Livity

Chapter Two

Word, Sound, Power
InI Theology

The ancient, most fervent, highly profound, and indulgent of all symbols is the human body. The Kehmetians, Greeks, Persians, Romans, and Hindus, considered a philosophical analysis of man's triune nature to be an irreducible, indispensable, part of social and religious training. The Mysteries of every culture taught that the laws, elements, and powers of the Iniverse, were epitomized in the human constitution; that everything which exists outside of man has its analogy within man.

The Iniverse, being immeasurable in its immensity and inconceivable in its profundity, was beyond mortal estimation. None, it was believed, could comprehend but part of the inaccessible splendor which was their source. When temporarily permeated with divine enthusiasm, man may transcend, for a brief moment, the limitations of his own personality and behold, in part, that celestial effulgence in which all creation is saturated. But even in his periods of greatest illumination, man himself is incapable of imprinting upon the substance of his rational soul, a perfect image of the multiform expression of Celestial activity.

Rastafari Livity

  Recognizing the futility of attempting to cope intelligibly with that which transcends the comprehension of the rationalizing faculties, the ancient priests and philosophers turned their attention from the inconceivable and incomprehensible, Divine Entity, to man himself; within the narrow confines of whose nature they found manifested all the mysteries of the external spheres. As a natural outgrowth of this Mystery System, a practice was fabricated and a secret society, theological system, in which God was considered as the Grand Man and, conversely, man the little god, was founded; bringing this teaching to commonality among them. Expanded on, in this Mystery, is that the Iniverse is regarded as a man, and man is the miniature Iniverse. The Greater Iniverse is termed the Macrocosm. The Great Body, and Divine Life controlling its functions, is called the Macroprosophus. Man's body, the individual human Iniverse, is termed the Microcosm, and the Divine Life controlling its functions is called Microprosophus. The Mysteries were primarily concerned with instructing initiates in the True relationship existing between the Macrocosm and the Microcosm, between Jah and Man. Accordingly, the key to these analogies, between the organs and functions of the Microcosmic man and those sublime celestial organs of the Macrocosmic Man, constituted the most prized possession of the early initiates. Contemporarily, in these days and times, InI now say that "ye are gods, children of the Most High God". A simple incantation infused with the wisdom of the Ancients as its source of power.

  Ages before idolatry was introduced into religion, the early priest caused the figure of man to be erected in the sanctuary of the temple. This human image symbolized the Divine Power in all of its intricate manifestations. Thus, the priests of antiquity knew that man, as a symbol of the image and likeness of Jah, is a study, a science, and a textbook, through which they learned to Overstand the greater, and more abstruse, mysteries of the Most High; and the Celestial scheme of which InI am a part of. After ages of research, man became a mass of intricate symbolic figures. Every part of him has its secret meaning. The measurements of man, therefore, formed a basic standard; by means of which it was possible to measure all parts of the Cosmos. It is a glorious composite emblem of all the knowledge possessed by the mavens, sages and gurus.

  Proceeding from the hypothesis of the first theologians, that man is actually fashioned in the image and likeness of Jah, the initiated minds of the past ages erected the stupendous structure of theology upon the foundation of the human body. Religion of today is almost completely ignorant of the fact that

Rastafari Livity

the science of Biology is an offshoot of the doctrines and tenets that are derived from the human body as their fountainhead. Most of the codes, statutes, laws, and commands, believed by modern sages and mavens, to have been direct revelations from Divinity, are in reality the reaping of ages of patient delving into the intricacies of the human constitution, and the infinite sublime wonders revealed by such a study.

The Ancient Sages divided man into three separate bodies. According to InI mystics, there are three lights, one for each body and the world in which it inhabits; truly analogous to the three centers of Life in each individual constitution. These three lights are the Spiritual Sun, the Sapient Sun, and the Material Sun. The Spiritual Sun nascents the Power of Jah, InI Father; The Sapient Sun radiates the Life of God, the Son; and the Material Sun is the Vehicle of Manifestation for Jah's Holy Spirit. Man's nature was also divided by the Mystics, into three distinct parts: Spirit, Soul, and Body. InI physical body is unfolded and vitalized by the Material Sun; InI Spiritual Nature is Illuminated by the Spiritual Sun; and InI Intelligent Nature is redeemed by the True Light of Grace, the Sapient Sun. This is Rastafari's Circadian Rhythm of the Trinity. InI renews InI Heights daily, never digressing to that former state of blindness.

Not only does Rastafari have this Diurnal State of Conscious Ability, but Rastafari has an annual pilgrimage, during which time InI subjectively pass successively through the teaching, directions, and Heights of the Twelve Celestial Houses of the Heavens; remaining in each for a Meditative Thirty Days. Added to these is a Third Path of contemplative travel, which is called the "Precession of the Equinoxes". On this path InI retrograde around the Zodiac through the Twelve signs. This is a path that is taught to travel one degree every seventy-two years, but since Rastafari knows that "All Time Exists Simultaneously", InI psychologically and mentally, travel this path one degree every seventy-two days, or seventy-two hours, depending on what the observance or reverence is about. This a path of Prophecy, Oneiromancy, Third Eye Revelations, Assuming the Essence of, or Triumphing Over that sign and its influences. Thus, InI perceives within the Perigee of a Bull in Taurus, Lion in Leo, Archer in Sagittarius, or Fish in Pisces, etc. etc.

Rastafari Livity

And this is just a fraction of the teachings of Rastafari's Heights, which to those who knoweth not is foolishness, but to InI who knoweth it is the Power of Jah Rastafari, who Liveth and Reigneth For-Iver.

H.I.M.'s Energy is Pervasive, Permeating all of Creation. A careful analysis of the religious systems of antiquity uncovers much evidence, of the fact, that its priests served this same Energy; and that their Supreme Being was, in every case, the Divine Light Personified that InI know as Jah Rastafari, Haile Selassie I. All the Gods of antiquity resolved themselves into this Energy, sometimes itself as God, or sometimes as an emblem, or Shekinah, of that higher principle; known by the description of the Creative Being, Most High, All Powerful, All Knowing, etc. This Energy is also known as the "Golden Mean". In society, it is the ethical midpoint between unethical extremes.

The Spirit is the center of man, his core, his sun. And so, what the sun is to InI solar system, the spirit is to the body of man; for his natures, organs, and functions are as planets surrounding the central and eternal Life, and living upon its emanations. The power that the Spirit provides in man is divided into three parts, which are termed the "Threefold Human Spirit" of man. All three of these "Spiritual Natures" are said to be radiant and transcendent. United, they form the Divinity in man. Man's threefold lower nature (consisting of his physical organism, his emotional nature, and his mental faculties) reflects the light of his threefold divinity, and bears witness of it in the manifest world. Man's three bodies are Astral, symbolized by an upright triangle; his threefold spiritual nature by an inverted triangle. These two triangles, when United in the form of a six-pointed star, is called "the Star of David", "the Signet of Solomon", and are more commonly known today as "the Star of Zion". These symbolize the spiritual and material universes linked together in the constitution of Man, who partakes of both Nature and Divinity.

Because of its scarcity, beauty, reflectivity and resplendence, gold has been prized, throughout history, more eagerly than any other thing. It does not rust or tarnish, which makes it a splendid representation of Divinity. The golden ornaments used by priest craft of the various world religions are subtle

Rastafari Livity

references to the Power, Energy, and Light of the "unseen". This is He who "Rastafari Extols As Jah". He is known by many manifestations, but has the same origin and reverence. The crowns of kings announce this reverence. Many of the ancient prophets, philosophers, and dignitaries carried a scepter, the upper end of which bore a representation of the Power of which the gold symbolized. One would be hard pressed to find any sacred or religious item, ornament, utensil, or object, in ancient times, that wasn't made of Gold; in order to represent the Holy Presence of the Divine, while here on earth. And now, in Rastafari, Gold as a concept, an ideal, a height, and a principle, is being carried forward to new territories of Man's thinking, behaviors, and speech. Bringing the "Golden Mean" into full manifest operation. For INI are "keepers of the light" with New Visions, but same meanings.

    Today, InI know more about the human body, and man as a whole, than InI Ancients could have ever wrote to INI. This knowledge is both enlightening and frightening, because man does all sorts of things with his knowledge. InI, as Rastafari, must be contemporary with this knowledge, and lift up its purpose to the benefit of the people. The science and physics of Man and His genome, can reveal Heights of Prophecy under the study and meditation of them. The other sciences will also benefit InI, because in studying nature, through the sciences, InI gain more knowledge of JAH's mystery, and His Direction for InI.

Chapter Three

HISTORY OF H.I.M.

    As any Rastafari of considerable study and elevation knows, the history of Rastafari nascented as the Primus Movement of Mind in its contact with Life Manifested. This Pure Essence of Man is the representation of Jah's Inner Dwelling. It is the Harmonious Consciousness that is created with Wisdom; it's idealized, and produces a plan of works that, once carried out, causes the ego, or will, to adhere to Wisdom faithfully.

    Rastafari in His Original Manifestation is Spiritual, Mystical, Illumination. The Spirit breathes with H.I.M. Itinually. The infusion of Truth Welding Heights and Knowledge grants H.I.M. Superior Overstanding that InI can at once master & apply. This is the Edenic Covenant, one of eight, and the highest one that man can reach in his flesh.

    But the Edenic Covenant is not where InI most recent and contemporary history is derived. It is not where this necessity of the "Age of Aquarius" stamps its certification. The history that is the necessity of Aquarius is certifiable, attested to, documented, and researchable for anyone with the simplest desire to do so. InI will expound and explicate this ecumenical history known today as

 *Rastafari Livity*

Rastafari.

This "Now" aspect of Rastafari nascents from Ethiopia, via Jamaica. Its Genesis is in His Imperial Majesty, Haile Selassie, The First, of Ethiopia. His Imperial Majesty's advent was as Lij Tafari Makonnen, born on the 16th of Hamle 1884, Ethiopic calendar (July 23, 1892, Gregorian calendar), in the village of Ejarsa Goro, in the Harar Provence. His mother was Woizero Yeshimebet Ali Abajifar, daughter of the renown Ormo ruler of the Wollo Provence, Dejazmach Ali Abajifar. His father was Ras Makonnen Woldemikael Gudessa, the then Govenor of Harar. Ras Makonnen was also a General, in military ranking, and played a key roll in the first Italo-Ethiopian war at the Battle of Adwa. His Imperial Majesty, Haile Selassie the first, inherited his Imperial Blood through his paternal grandmother, Princess Tenagenework Sahle Selassie, who was an aunt of Emperor Menelik II.

His Imperial Majesty became Dejazmach (literally "commander of the gate," a title equivalent to the Western "count") at the age of 13, on Thikimt 22, 1898 (November 1, 1905). He had received His educational instructions in Harar from Abba Samuel Wolde Kahin, an Ethiopian Capuchin Monk, and from Dr. Vitalier, a surgeon from Guadeloupe, and that ensured that H.I.M. would be well prepared for such a position. H.I.M. was always known for his insight and advance critical thinking ability as a youth. H.I.M. assumed the titular governorship of Selale in 1899 (1906), and then in 1900 (1907) was appointed governor over part of the province of Sidamo. All the while H.I.M. continued His studies in religion, academics, liberal arts, and fine arts.

In between 1903 and 1904 (1910 and 1911) H.I.M. was made governor of Harar, finally assuming the position of His Father, Ras Makonnen Woldemikael Gudessa, who had passed forward at Kulibi in 1899 (1906). This very special time for H.I.M. was also Blessed by H.IM.'s Marriage to Empress Mennen, who was then known as Mennen Asfew of Anbassel, niece of the heir to the throne, at that time, Lij Iyasu.

From 1906 (1913) to 1909 (1916) Lij Iyasu, or Iyasu V, was the designated but uncrowned Emperor of the Ethiopian Empire. His inclination for scandalous behavior and disrespectful attitude, towards the nobles at the court of his grandfather, Menelik II, damaged his reputation. His never being anointed Emperor was due to his claiming descent from the Islamic Prophet Muhammad, exchanging some of the Ethiopic Flags for Islamic versions, and finally, wanting to

Rastafari Livity

sit on the Throne of Ethiopia as a Muslim. Soon, on Meskerem 17, 1909 (September 27, 1916) he was deposed.

In replacing Iyasu, Wayzaro Zewditu, the daughter of Menelik II and aunt of Iyasu, became Queen Empress Zewditu, and H.I.M. was elevated to Crown Prince and Regent Plenipotentiary, His Highness, Ras Tafari Makonnen. In the arrangement of power, H.I.M., as H.H. Ras Tafari Makonnen, accepted the role of Inderase (Regent) and became the de facto (in reality or fact; actually) ruler of the Ethiopian Empire. On or about Nehasie 1920 (August 1928), the nobles and ministers living in Addis Abadu, as well as the army commanders and all men holding office, reached a unanimous agreement, and declared, that Empress Zewditu should have H.H. Crown Prince Tafari Makonnen proclaimed Negus (King) and have H.I.M. carry out, on His Sole Authority, any government business without having to consult anyone. H.I.M. felt a little awkward about this and felt that it was very difficult because once proclaimed Negus (King) of some large part of Ethiopia, He could not go there or else the Empress would need another Regent Plenipotentiary. As Negus (King) He could scarcely reside at Addis Ababa, for it was not customary for two Kings, in this case one being a Queen, to reside in one city. H.I.M. asked for the matter to be dropped, but the nobles, ministers, army commanders, and men of office sent back word saying: "We cannot go back on it, for the reason we have acted was that we were mindful of the honor of our realm and the benefit and peace of our people, without favoring anyone". So, with popular, respected, police, and military support Empress Zewditu approved for H.H. Crown Prince, Tafari Makonnen to be proclaimed Negus (King) of The Ethiopian Empire Meskerem 27, 1921 (October 7, 1928), receiving the Crown from Empress Zewditu.

After being chosen as heir to the throne, H.I.M. patiently carried out the work and duties of government for fourteen (14) years. On Megabit. 24, 1922 (April 2, 1930) Empress Zewditu passed forward, and consequently, on the next day Megabit 25, (April 3, 1930), prophecy ranged high that, His Highness Negus Tafari Makonnen be now declared Negus Negestze Ityoppy (King of Kings of Ethiopia).

According to ancient practices, as regards the succession of throne and crown, at a time when Ethiopia lived in isolation, and before she had established relations with foreign countries, the prevailing custom had been, at the demise of the Emperor, for his death to remain carefully unannounced. They would either place his son and heir on the throne, and crown him immediately, that

Rastafari Livity

very day; announcing the death of the King and give a ceremonial burial after the son's reign and coronation had been announced; or at the demise of the Emperor, the officers of the royal household would take him clandestinely and bury him, before anyone could hear about it, and on the very next day would place his son and heir on the throne. After they had conducted the royal installation service and crowned him, the death of the father and new reign of the son would be announced by proclamation at the same time.

But at this time of H.I.M., Ethiopia had concluded treaties of commerce and friendship with twelve foreign countries, had entered the League of Nations, and established firm friendly relations. So it was now proper, in accordance with the practice of the most civilized governments, in the case of their coronations, to invite all of the countries which had set up legations and consulates in Ethiopia. Also, the princes and nobles and all the headmen, the priors of monasteries, and deans of cathedrals were now all Joyously able to participate in H.I.M.'s coronation. Therefore, it was arranged for the coronation to be postponed for seven months to, Thikimit 23,1923 (November 2, 1930).

The invited foreign envoys begin to arrive between Thikimit 8th and 20th (Oct. 18-30), from such places as England, Italy, Belgium, Sweden, the Netherlands, Japan, Egypt, France, U.S.A., Germany, Greece, Turkey, and Poland. The emissaries of those Nations were: H.R.H. The Duke of Gloucester, envoy of H.M. the King of England; H.R.H. the Prince of Udine, envoy of H.M. the King of Italy; H.E.M. Gerard, envoy of H.M. the King of the Belgians; H.E. Baron H.K.C. Bildt, envoy of H.M. the King of Sweden; H.E. Jonkheer Hendrik Maurits van Haersma de With, envoy of H.I.M. the Queen of the Netherlands; H.E.M. Isaburo Yoshida, envoy of H.M. the Emperor of Japan; H.E. Muhammad Tawfiq Nasim Pasha, envoy of H.M. the King of Egypt; H.E. Marshal Franchet d'Esperey, envoy of the French Republic; H.E. Mr. H.M. Jacoby, envoy of the U.S.A.; H.E. Baron von Waldthausen, envoy of the Greek Republic; H.E. Muhittin Pasa, envoy of the Turkish Republic, and H.E. Count Dzieduszycki, envoy of the Polish Republic.

Following ancient traditions, 49 bishops and priests, in groups of seven, in seven corners of the cathedral, chanted continually, nine Psalms of David for seven days and nights, prior to the coronation.

On November 1, the eve of the coronation, the Emperor inaugurated a statue to the great Emperor Menelik II. The honor of unveiling went to the Duke of Gloucester; the envoy of the King of England. That same evening, the Imperial

Rastafari Livity

vestments and ornaments were taken, in a great parade, to the Royal Church of St. George, and consigned to the Archbishop who prayed over them all night. The Cathedral of St. George is a magnificent structure, built during the reign of Emperor Menelik II, and was the scene of the Crowning of Empress Zewditu in 1916. His Imperial Majesty and His family entered that church at midnight for a night of prayer.

As Sunday, November 2, dawn cleared, all in Addis Ababa began to prepare for the impressive event of the morning. The Conquering Lion of the Tribe of Judah, Ras Tafari Makonnen, now Haile Selassie 1st, and His Empress, Mennen Asfew of Anbassel, had just completed a night of prayer and devotion at the Most High's Altar, within St. George's Cathedral. The forty-nine bishops and priests of this ancient Orthodox Christian Nation, in those groups of seven, had held a place for seven days and nights, in the seven corners of the National Cathedral, and chanted, without ceasing, nine Psalms of David. They were then joined by hundreds more, and through the early morning the chanting of praises continued; accompanied by the dancing of the priests with their great pulsating drums. The whole scene is suggestive of the Ancient Judaic rites which were in use at the time of King David, who danced before the Ark of the Covenant.

Proceeded by waving incense burners, His Imperial Majesty, attired in white silk communion robes, entered the ceremonial hall with an escort of aides and clergy.

More than 700 guests and officials were in attendance, on Thikimit 23, 1923 (November 2, 1930), to witness this ancient Hebraic-Christian coronation ceremony. Lion-maned chieftains were interspersed among the foreign guest and dignitaries, each according to rank and station. Hundreds of priests joined the original group, resplendent in their colorful ceremonial robes, bearing crosses and censers.

Before the Royal Ritual began, His Imperial Majesty, Haile Selassie, whose name is Anglicized as Power of the Holy Trinity, is approached by the Archbishop, His- Holiness, Abuna Qerillos, with a Holy Bible, bound in gold, and is asked to pledge the following four-point oath: "To strengthen and defend the Orthodox Faith, and to keep, without disturbance, the laws and ordinances which the Orthodox Tewahedo Church has laid down".

"To safeguard the entire Ethiopian realm and people in accordance with the established laws and ordinances of the Council."

Rastafari Livity

"To assist with the establishment of schools in Ethiopia where secular and spiritual education would be developed, and the gospels would be preached for developing the Spiritual and Material welfare of her subjects".

The Emperor then affirms verbally, and in writing, that He is willing to fulfill His duties as Ruler. This concluded the swearing-in ceremony.

The thrilling confirmation is then altered by the throaty voice of His Holiness the Abuna Qerillos saying: "Ye princes and Ministers, Ye Nobles and Chiefs of the Army, Ye Soldiers and People of Ethiopia, and Ye Doctors and Chiefs of the Clergy, Ye Professors and Priests, look Ye upon Our Emperor Haile Selassie the First, descended from the Dynasty of Menelik the First, who was born of Solomon and the Queen of Sheba, Makeda. A Dynasty perpetuated without interruption from the time of King Handady 179-178 to our times".

Next, the Abuna recites the prayer of the covenant. After which, the choir, with the drums and harps accompaniments, chant the 48th Psalm. Chanting and prayers to the God of gods rise from a multitude of priestly throats and reverberate from the lofty ceiling of the Cathedral.

During this Interval, abbots from various monasteries bring the Royal Articles one by one, handing them to the six bishops, with the solemn rites and blessings of the High Ethiopian Clergy, who were assigned by the Archbishop to the coronation service. The bishops, in turn, pass the articles to the Abuna, to be blessed. The objects were returned to the respective bishops who then presented them to His Imperial Majesty, reciting appropriate lines.

His Imperial Majesty, with each of the seven ornaments, is anointed on the head, brow, and shoulders, with seven differently scented ointments (oils) of ancient prescription. H.I.M. received the Gold-Embroidered Scarlet Robes. He is vested with the Jeweled Sword along with this exhortation. "May you be enabled, with this sword, to punish the wicked and protect the righteous". This is followed with the bestowal of the Imperial Scepter of Ivory and Gold, the Golden Orb (Globe), a Diamond encrusted ring, and two Traditional Lances (spears) Filigreed in Gold, in token of His position and responsibility.

Following Ancient Customs of Ethiopia and Israel, as when Samuel anointed David, Zadok and Nathan anointed Solomon, and Azariyus anointed Menelik I, so the Abuna anointed His Imperial Majesty's Head with the Oil of Kingship; seven differently scented ointments of ancient prescription on the now Imperial Head, Brow, and Shoulders. The Abuna places upon H.I.M. the "Triple

Rastafari Livity

Crown," and the Archbishop concludes the Regal Anointing with the words: "That God may make this Crown a Crown of Sanctity and Glory. That, by the Blessings which we have given you, may you have an Unshaken Faith and a Pure Heart, in order that you may inherit the "Crown Eternal", So be it".

The centuries seemed to have slipped suddenly backward into a Biblical Time of Rituals. "For King Ras Tafari Makonnen, of the lineage of King David, King Solomon, and Emperor Menelik 1 (the first), Anointed As His Imperial Majesty Haile Selassie 1 (the First) had been Crowned the 225th Emperor of Ethiopia."

The Crown Prince, Asafa Wossen, removed his coronet and on bended knee pledged his allegiance, service, and support, to his Father, Lord, and King, His Imperial Majesty, Haile Selassie the First.

The Empress and Her Ladies of Honor then enter the sanctuary from the right side, and she takes Her throne to the right of His Imperial Majesty for Her coronation. It was determined that the Abuna is to place the Crown on Her head and the Ring upon Her Majesty's finger, without the Regal Anointing, on the same day of the Emperor's coronation. This breaks tradition and sets a historical precedent as the earlier practice, of ancient times, was for her to be Crowned on the third day after the coronation of the Emperor, in the palace and not in the church.

The final part of the ceremony is a tour of the Cathedral by their Imperial Majesties, escorted by the bishops and priests, the princes and dignitaries, assistants and others, carrying palm branches and chanting, "Blessed be the King".

The assembly applauded their greeting, and the visiting naval band played the National Anthem, while outside cannons roared a 101 guns salute. The procession continued on to Addis Ababa Streets, where thousands of well-wishers wildly cheered for the Royal Family. Cheer after cheer came from the thousands of subjects massed in the vicinity of the cathedral.

The coronation drew to a close with their Majesties visiting the other churches in the city to give thanks and praises.

The tangible components, and elements, of H.I.M.'s eventual Coronation are what InI have just disclosed. Let's now look into the prophesies and revelations that surrounded H.I.M.'s actual Coronation, and the essence of what

Rastafari Livity

it all should mean to InI.

There was a prophecy spoken of, prior to H.I.M. 's birth, by a well-known Muslim Imam. He prophesied that His Imperial Majesty would be born in order to get rid of the sour and remove the unpleasant, and that He would judge the poor and the noble. In a mystical ritual, the Imam planted a Koso tree on the compound of the Ejarso, St. Mary's Church. The Koso tree is very bitter tasting, but is well known as a cure for a diseased stomach, so as The Koso tree is a cure for the stomach, H.I.M. is the cure for human suffering. It is said that the Imam planted H.I.M.'s umbilical cord under this Koso tree. The people of Ejarso, upon completion of the planting, asked the Imam "What is this"? He explained that "the child born today, unto Ras Makonnen, will be a great man. He will rule over Ethiopia and be the pride of Africa. He will give solutions to our problems and give fair judgment".

What gives this particular prophecy meritorious attention is that Islam contributes to Ethiopia's strong, diverse, and spiritual permeation. Islam has been in and around Ethiopia for its entire existence, and the best of Islam is always received.

Let us explain the history of this auspicious and serendipitous coalescing:

Because of the continuous and unrelenting persecution of Quraish towards the Muslims, it was next to impossible for any among them to publicly declare his acceptance of the faith, much less call others to Islam. When this continued for a long while, the nobles of Quraish went to Muhammad's uncle Abu-Talib and attempted to bribe him to renounce his protection of Muhammad (PBUH). When this did not succeed, they went to Muhammad directly and attempted to bribe him with wealth, leadership, nobility, and to appoint him as their leader, if he would but renounce his message. He refused. Now when the torture of Quraish became unbearable, Muhammad (PBUH) authorized his companions to emigrate to Ethiopia (Abyssinia). At this point, eighty-three Muslims fled Makkah and traveled to Ethiopia. When the nobles of Quraish saw that the Muslims had found a reprieve from their torture and abuse in Abyssinia, and that they were allowed to practice their religion freely there, these nobles decided to send a delegation to King Armah II of Abyssinia; consisting of Abdullah, the son of Rabia and Amr, the son of Altas; and with them they sent

Rastafari Livity

many gifts for the King and his Generals. When this delegation arrived in Abyssinia, they first presented their gifts to the King's generals and received passage to speak to the King. When they stood before the King they said: "There has come to your land a scrapping lot of our most ignorant juveniles. They have departed from the religion of their fathers and have not accepted your religion, rather, they have invented a completely new religion which neither we nor you have heard of before. The nobles among their people, their fathers, their uncles, and their clan have sent to you to return them to them, for they are best acquainted with them and closer in bond to them." The King's officers then spoke up saying: "They have spoken the truth oh King so let us return them to their people." Upon hearing this, the King became very angry and refused to accept their words or to return those who had sought sanctuary with him to this delegation. He then commanded that the Muslims be assembled before him as well as His Bishops.

When they had all assembled before him, he asked the Muslims: "What is this religion which has caused you to relinquish the religion of your fathers and not to accept our religion nor any of these other faiths?" Ja' far the son of Abu-Talib, the cousin of Muhammad (PBUH) then arose and said: "O King Armah II of Abyssinia, we used to be a people of ignorance, worshipping idols, eating dead animals, performing indecencies, casting off family bonds, doing evil to our neighbors, and the strong among us would eat the weak. This remained our common trait until God sent to us a messenger. We knew his ancestry, his truthfulness, his trustworthiness, and his chastity. He called us to Allah that we might worship Him alone and forsake all that which we had been worshipping other than Him, of these stones and idols. He commanded us to be truthful in speech, to keep our trusts, to strengthen our family bonds, to be good to our neighbors, to avoid the prohibitions and blood, and to avoid all indecencies, lying, theft of the orphan's money, and the slander of chaste women. He further commanded us to worship Allah alone, not associating anything in worship with Him. He commanded us to pray, pay charity, and fast (and he listed for him the requirements of Islam). So we believe him, accepted his message, and followed him in that which he received from Allah, worshipping Allah alone, not associating any partners with Him, refraining from all prohibitions, and accepting all that which was made permissible for us. For this, our people greeted us with animosity and vindication. They tortured us and persecuted us in our religion in the hope that they might turn us from the worship of Allah to the worship of idols, and that we might accept that which we had accepted of our old evil

deeds. So when they overcame us, dealt unjustly with us, restricted us, and barred us from our religion, we fled to your land and chose you above all others, hoping for your sanctuary, and hoping that we would not fear injustice in your presence. "The King listened to Ja'far's words patiently and quietly then he said: "Do you have with you any of that which your companion has brought to you?" Ja'far replied "Yes." The King said: "Then recite it before me." So Ja' far recited to him the verses of the chapter of Maryam (chapter 19). When the King heard these verses, he wept till he soaked his beard, and with him, his Bishops also wept. The King then said: "Verily, this and that which was brought by Yeshua (Jesus) have indeed come from the same burning light." He then turned to the emissaries of Quraish and said to them: "Return to your people, for I shall never deliver them to you." The next morning, Amr the son of Al-Aas returned to King Armah II and said: "They say a most monstrous thing regarding Jesus the son of Mary." Ja' far the son of Abu-Talib replied: "We say in his regard that which our prophet says: That he was the servant of God and his messenger, a spirit from Him, and His Word which He bestowed upon Mary the chaste, the pure." Upon hearing this the king struck the ground with his hand and lifted up a stick. He then said, "Verily, Jesus the son of Mary did not surpass what you have just said even so much as this stick." The King granted the Muslims sanctuary and the emissaries of Quraish returned with empty hands. This King of Ethiopia later passed away during the lifetime of Muhammad (PBUH). When Muhammad learned of his death, he commanded the Muslims to assemble for a congregational "prayer upon the deceased" (funeral prayer) on King Armah's II behalf.

But Islam wasn't alone in prophesying about H.I.M. 's birth. After eight (8) stillbirths, Lady Yeshimebet, H.I.M.'s mother, was now pregnant for the ninth (9th) time. As the pregnancy of the wife of Ras Makonnen, ruler of Harar, was heard, many religious figures prophesied that the pregnancy of Lady Yeshimebet, this time, was different. They told that He Will Live, and that the child must be separated from His mother upon His birth, and taken to another place. They also prophesied about the future of the child being a ruler and server of His people. When Ras Makonnen heard the prophecies, he did not give much value. He said "It is God that gives or denies a child. So why should we interfere with His Work, and separate mother and child". He, however, was desperate to have a child, so

Rastafari Livity

it did not take him long to agree to do whatever was needed.

The presentation to Ras Makonnen, concerning why he should do the things told to him, came from the science of astrology. Understanding that H.I.M. would be born on the very first day of Leo, meant that a host of things, needing preparation, would have to been done, with "True Assurance", in order for H.I.M. to become King of Kings, Lord of Lords, Conquering Lion of the Tribe of Judah. Remembering that Jah works, and realistically so, through the hands of Men.

The first thing that needed noting was what "duality" would H.I.M. possess here on earth? A duality is one of the classifications under which signs of the zodiac are grouped. A signs duality is either masculine or feminine, and H.I.M.'s duality is masculine. This is what creates, in H.I.M., the personality traits like being outer-directed, energetic, strong through action, and a bold presenter. These qualities are necessary for the peoples motivation, inspiration, and elevation into nation building.

H.I.M. prophetic Triplicity (element), is the Fire. This is how the sharp word will goeth out His mouth, and He will rule them with a rod of iron and will treadeth the winepress of the fierceness and wrath that will be called for by this world. H.I.M.'s judgment cannot be easily sundered by this world or any of its influences, therefore His triplicity has to be the Fire, so that a purification is maintained.

H.I.M. was also prophesied a quality called Quadruplicity that is "Fixed". This is where His persistence, single-mindedness, determination, and resourcefulness, that nascents from H.I.M., is filled with a "Spirit of Enthusiasm", and that "Spirit" is infused with teachings that are powerful, expansive and creative, generous and extravagant, and very deep in meaning.

He has to be "Fixed" in order to bring to fruition the "Life Changing Zeitgeist" needed by the people. He will have with Him that which is "Faithful and True," and it will always be done in Righteousness, through His "Fixed" quality.

Out of all the noble births of that calendar year, H.I.M. occupied a central status of Primus Inter Pares. This gave Him the appearance of a "Rising Sun" to

Rastafari Livity

the Priests and People. They knew that He carried with Him vitality and authority. This "Sun Symbol" illuminated His regal, brave, and dominating, nobility and pride. It also reveals the inheritance of His Forefather's "King David" Heart; for the Lord said unto Samuel, "Look not on his countenance, or on the height of his stature for the Lord seeth not as man seeth; for man looketh on the outward appearance, but the Lord looketh on the heart... then Samuel took the horn of oil, and anointed him in the midst of his brethren: and the Spirit of the Lord came upon David from that day forward. " On that day, David wasn't King of Israel in service and position, and that is where the prophecy of H.I.M.' s birth gets its strength in accuracy. Because, a King is a King long before the people, or other nations, know him to be. A king is a king from Jah's Authority, and is determined by Jah before the beginning of time.

    H.I.M.'s pictograph represents the heart, which is also the "Star of David". These, two of the same, symbolize the power derived from both the intellect and the emotions; the two strongest centers of the mind. It was reasoned that H.I.M.' s discipline would be mistaken for complacency by some foolish perceivers of His "I Will" presence of Truth. This would be the most visible of the prophecy known by those who would know H.I.M. The humility that H.I.M. displayed was unequaled for a ruler at that time. In those days, His meekness surpassed even the religious leaders; and all in authority never possessed that "Ivine Patience" that H.I.M instantly projected upon every interaction.

    H.I.M.'s prophecy also included that He would possess large ideas, humanitarian concepts, and the hopes, wishes, and higher aspirations of mankind. H.I.M. would be the "Living Blood Ruby" of humanity. Protecting against physical injury and harm, and ensuring faithfulness to the weak hearted. To those who would adhere to H.I.M., He would grant serenity of mind. His loyalty would be without question, as the "Living" and True "Blood Ruby" of Man, sought purely to create only that which would be for the betterment of Man.

    The status of the Priests, the conviction in, and details of, the prophecy, and Ras Makonnen's deep desire to have a child, especially a son, solidified H. H. to prepare and carry out all of the necessary requirements that would ensure H.I.M.'s right course and development towards the achievements of His Prophetic Potential.

Rastafari Livity

H.I.M. is prophecy manifest because Jah made the earth empty, and made it waste, and turned it upside down, and scattered abroad all the inhabitants thereof.

And it has been, as with the people, so with the priest; as with the servant, so with his master; as with the maid, so with her mistress; as with the buyer, so with the seller; as with the lender, so with the borrower; as with the taker of usury, so with the giver of usury to him.

The land has been utterly emptied, and utterly spoiled: for Jah has spoken this word. He has made it so.

The earth mourned and fades away, the world languishes and fades away, the haughty people of this world do languish in agony.

The earth is defiled under the inhabitants thereof; because they have transgressed the laws, changed the ordinances, and broken the everlasting covenant.

Jah's curses rose and devoured this world and they that dwell therein. Everything is desolate, and all things are burned in wicked desires, reprobated minds, and leaners on their own understandings.

The new wine mourns, the vine languisheth, all the merry-hearted do sigh. The mirth of tabrets ceaseth, the noise of them that rejoice ends, and the joy of the harp ceaseth.

Therefore, Jah manifested in Ras Tafari Makonnen, elevated to His Imperial Majesty Haile Selassie The 1st, and gives the Holy Spirit to all who are in need of One God, One Aim, One Destiny. And as one of the Elders spoke"... Weep not; Behold, the Lion of the Tribe of Judah, The Root of David, has prevailed to open the Book, and to loose the seven seals thereof...". And He came and took the book out of the Right Hand of Him that sat upon the Throne.

And when He had taken the Book, the Four beast, and Twenty-Four Elders fell down having every one of them harps, and golden vials full of odors, which are the prayers of saints. And they sang a "New Song", saying, "Thou art worthy to take the Book and to open the seals thereof and hast redeemed InI to Jah, by thy Blood, out of every kindred, and tongue, and people, and nation. And has made InI, unto Our God, Kings and Priests: and InI shall Reign on the earth."

Rastafari Livity

It is imperative that InI establish an elevation in the fundamental and factual nature of Rastafari. In InI's inception, many ideas were brought forth and manufactured to produce what was needed of the people; some flourished, while others did not do so well, hence the reasoning for a complete and clear fundamental teaching. H.I.M. has always embodied and expressed a singularity, and oneness, that no one could ever make separate; except in a limited and fallacious perception of H.I.M. The collective duty of man, that H.I.M. teaches InI, is one that man should use to accomplish great endeavors. It is in this same light that InI now present to InI, the clarity and realization, H.I.M.'s core, central, and fundamental belief, knowledge, and wisdom of coadunation, and the confluent characteristics that are produced by it, with the application of H.I.M.'s Rastafari Livity.

Rastafari Livity

Chapter Four

Rastafari Eldership/Timelines

Biblical and Religious prophecy was followed by the "Social Prophecy" of Marcus Garvey. Marcus Mosiah Garvey is Rastafari's Prophet comparable to John the Baptist. Many of the early Rastafari had started out as Garveyites, which were already teaching Black Nationalism, Black Separatism, and Pan-Africanism: a belief system that teaches that all Black People of the world should join in brotherhood and work to decolonize the African Continent.

Marcus Garvey promoted his cause of Black Pride throughout the 1930s. One of the most famous prophecies attributed to him involved the coronation of H.I.M. in the 1927 pronouncement: "Look to Africa, for there a King shall be Crowned".

This did nothing for the status quo, but it was particularly successful and influential among the lower-class blacks in Jamaica; in rural communities. This prophecy created hope for the hopeless, and gave strength to the downtrodden.

The enormous power and influence that Marcus Garvey had on the nascent of Rastafari was Phenomenal.

Rastafari Livity

Garvey's messages, philosophies, and ideals, are saturated throughout Rastafari. Marcus Garvey's travels, organizational abilities, and pioneering efforts established a basis, and a spirit, for foundational and fundamental Rastafari development. His direct campaigns to unify Africa, and to create a government of Black Rule, were truly groundbreaking for an African Diaspora who was decades from any mental, physiological, Liberation and/or Emancipation; and who were positioned as eye witnesses to the aggressiveness and violence done by the opposition of those ideals.

After this "Manifestation of Prophecy" and "Scriptural Fulfillment", the announcement to the world began. The Coronation created great publicity throughout the world through two consecutive Time Magazine articles and two National Geographic issues. Anyone who sought the highest in spiritual and mystical phenomena was immediately triggered to turn their attention to Ethiopia and InI Emperor, His Imperial Majesty, Haile Selassie The 1st, King of Kings, Lord of Lords, Conquering Lion of the Tribe of Judah, and Elect of Jah.

The emergence of Rastafari came over the next few years. InI Three Elders, who were all overseas and away from the Jamaican, Babylonian, mental corruption, well received the Blowing of the Trumpet at H.I.M.'s Coronation.

Elder Leonard P. Howell began spreading the news in Kingston. Elder Archibald Dunkley landed at Port Antonio and began his teachings. Around 1933, he relocated to Kingston where the "King of King's Ethiopian Mission" was founded. Elder Joseph Hibbert returned from Costa Rica in 1931 and began spreading the Heights of InI Emperor's divinity in the Benoah district, Saint Andrew Parish, through his own ministry, called Ethiopian Coptic Faith.

Elder Leonard P. Howell began Rastafari writings with The Promise Key. He was overwhelmed by the spiritual significance of the coronation and searched the Bible for the True Meaning and Answers of it. He saw too many parallels, consistencies, and what others may call or consider coincidences, to ignore as such, or happenstances. He is the "First Rasta" who proclaimed that H.I.M., Haile Selassie the first, of Ethiopia is InI True Head of Creation and Christ in His Kingly Character. InI say "First Rasta" because persecution, ridicule, and incarceration came to the Elder for his knowledge of the Truth with Actions. InI know that, as Rastafari, those three things are common place, especially since Rastafari denounces European Kings and Kingdoms. Elder Leonard P. Howell was charged, at several different times, with sedition, spending time in jail and in an

Rastafari Livity

asylum. He most definitively revealed the ways of Rastafari in Babylon, and Babylon's thoughts towards and treatment of Rastafari.

Upon his release, Elder Leonard Howell formed a commune in St. Catherine, Jamaica, called Pinnacle, which grew to a population of 2000 people. The Jamaican government razed this community, because it believed it to be on government land, and not free land. It considered the community squatters and illegal inhabitants, and they were inimical towards them.

From this point, InI received the Theocratic Priesthood and Livity Order of Nyabinghi, InI Eldest Mansion and /or House; Bobo Shanti, founded by Prince Emanuel Charles Edwards, in Jamaica, in the 1950's; and The Twelve Tribes of Israel, founded in 1968 by Dr. Vernon "Prophet Gad" Carrington. These three laid the Foundation for all future Rastafari thought, theology, outlook, and development.

Timelines

1. Leonard Percival Howell- June 16, 1898-Feb. 25,1981 (born into Angilican) Gangunguru Maragh, G.G. Maragh = Gyan-wisdom; gun-virtue or talent; guru-teacher; Maragh-great Kings
    - Served as a soldier in Panama.
    - Visited New York several times beginning in 1918
    - Joined U.S. Army Transport Service as a cook
    - Discharged in 1923, from the military
    - Returned to Jamaica, possibly deported, by 1932 at 34 yrs. old
    - Moved to St. Thomas in Feb. of 1933
    - Arrested in 1934 for sedition, stemming from a speech given at Seaforth in front of 300 people, Dec. 10, 1933. The trial was on March 13, 1934, where he declared His Imperial Majesty, Haile Selassie 1, is The Messiah returned.
    - Sentenced to two years.
    - Founded The Ethiopian Salvation Society in 1937
    - Sent to Bellevue Mental Asylum for the "Promised Key"
    - Settled Pinnacle Estate in Sligoville St. Catherine, 1940

Rastafari Livity

- Arrested again in 1943, sentenced to two years, released in 1945
- 1954 the military invaded and almost destroyed Pinnacle
- 1958 Pinnacle cleared out by police

2. Henry Archibald Dunkley-A seaman for the United Fruit Company
   - Arrived in Port Antonio between 1930-1931. Started ministry
   - Moved to Kingston in 1933
   - Imprisoned a number of times between 1934-1935
   - Foundation member of Ethiopian World Federation

3. Joseph Nathaniel Hibbert- The Scientists; 1894-Sept. 18, 1986
   - At 17, moved to Costa Rica and spent 20 years as a farmer
   - Became member of Ancient Order of Ethiopia Masonic Lodge
   - Came from Costa Rica in 1931. Started ministry in St. Andrew
   - Founded the Ethiopian Coptic Faith
   - Help Found the Ethiopian World Federation first chapter, number 17, with a Brother Paul Earlington.
   - In 1971, was named "Spiritual Organizer", by Abuna Laike Mandefro called Archbishop Abuna Yesehaq Archbishop of the Western Hemisphere and South Africa, of the Ethiopian Orthodox Church.

4. Robert Hinds-Bedwardite, Garveyite
   - Imprisoned in 1921 with Bedward
   - Arrested 12 or more times for his ministry
   - Established King of Kings Mission headquarters; 82 N. St. and 6 Law St.
   - Leader and Shepherd, had twelve male officers, twelve water-mothers, every man given a staff.
   - Two feast days-Ethiopian New Year & Emancipation Day
   - Implemented fasting, up to three days, before feasts
   - Passover lasted 14 days, roasted lamb or goat, no broken bones, no leavened bread, whatever wasn't eaten was burned
   - Established "Cabinet" of seven of the most faithful and promising
   - Baptismal
   - Established Guards

Rastafari Livity

Chapter Five

The Nazirite Vow

    The most distinguishing aspect of Rastafari is his Nazirite Vow. The Nazirite Vow is a Vow in which the Man or Wombman "Separates themselves unto JAH… All the days of the vow of his separation there shall no razor come upon his head: until the days be fulfilled, in the which he separated himself unto the Lord, he shall be holy, and shall let the locks of his head grow" (Numbers 6:5). Many of the other aspects of the Nazirite Vow aren't necessarily visible, or detectable: the non-drinking of strong drink, neither drinking of any liquor, not coming at any dead body, being separate to the Lord in joy, not to eat moist grapes, or dried, nor anything that is made of the vine tree, could all be done without the knowledge or witnessing of. Therefore, in Rastafari, the locks are a sure sign of the Nazirite Vow.

    Now, whereas it is True that one does not have to be dread, or have locks, to be "Rasta", it is impossible to be a Nazirite without them. The Nazirite and Priesthood require Locks without compromise. Also, you can be "A Priest" without locks, but a Nazirite Priest as spoken of in Leviticus 21: 4-6 or Ezekiel 44:

15-31 cannot be carried out "Rightly" without Locks. These are "High Priest of Rastafari", that hold and carry forth the "Torch and Light" of JAH RASTAFARI, as the vessel and emissary of His Imperial Majesty Haile Selassie The First. The Nazirite Vow is an aspect of the Hebraic Element in Rastafari that has no equal, no derivatives, no deviations, nothing but a strict carrying out of duty, obligation and responsibility.

There are also those who have locks, carry locks, and wear locks who have not made a Nazirite Vow, or any vow. Some are just fashion focused, some recognize locks as a form of rebelliousness for them, and others feel a sense of pride in just having their locks. With these individuals, it is difficult to know if they are a Rastafari Nazirite or not. The person themselves would have to either confirm or deny, and then his expressions would certify.

Also, InI have some Rastafari that claim that their locks are worn by their hearts. In this circumstance, speech, actions, duty, and responsibilities would, therefore, confirm or deny the presence of locks, subjectivity. The Vow's wording, that say, "...There shall none be defiled for the dead among his people," Leviticus 21: 1; "All the days that he separateth himself unto the Lord he shall come at no dead body", Numbers 6:6; and "And they shall come at no dead person to defile themselves...", Ezekiel 44:25, are very clear on how the Rastafari Nazirite is to be in his environment, and implied in his diet. Death is not applicable, and dead things aren't interacted with. In the beginning of Rastafari, there were InI bearded elders who sought to reflect the manifest image of H.I.M. They were compelled to look like H.I.M.; using the logic that that would bring them closer in Spiritual Proximity, but that was just their belief and conviction.

It has often been suggested, that the first Rasta Locksmen were copied from the 1953 Kenya Mau Mau insurgents, who grew their "dreaded locks" while hiding, in gurella warfare tactics, in the mountains. These locksmen appeared in newsreels and other print publications that reached Jamaica. Another tale of the origin of "locksmen" have them nascenting out of a subgroup of Blacks in 1949 known as Youth Black Faith. Either story will suffice; For it is not truly known how locks were introduced into Rastafari, nor is it a necessary aspect.

One thing is for certain though, the Nazirite Vow is predominantly carried out by Rastafari. As far as the Judeo-Christian-Islamic Abrahamic religions go, Rastafari fills a massive void that had been growing for a millennium or more.

Rastafari Livity

    The Nazirite of Rastafari is they that shall teach the people the "difference" between the holy and profane, and cause them to discern between the unclean and the clean. And in controversy they shall stand in judgment; and they shall judge it according to H.I.M.'s judgments; and they shall keep H.I.M.'s laws and statutes in all H.I.M.'s assemblies; and they shall hallow H.I.M.'s Sabbaths.

    Now specifically concerning Ezekiel 44, InI find that there is a designation between the Priesthood. One is for the People. One is for JAH. The One for the People is readily known as what has been described thus far. But the Priest unto JAH are not readily known, even by other Priest.

    The Priest unto Jah minister unto H.I.M. InI stand before H.I.M. (four and twenty elders) For-Iver. InI are entered into H.I.M.'s Sanctuary, immersed in its manifestation, its Reality. InI are Near H.I.M.'s Table, receptive, accepting of its Bounty, Ministering unto H.I.M. what has already been mystically given; incomprehensible beyond the Table and Sanctuary, and only for those who hear and see. InI have and keep the charge, maintaining the balance, surety, and Truth of Law. The people will not just be sanctified by InI Heights of Truth. InI am the vessel of H.I.M.'s Omnification.

    When and what InI present will be the Iver Renewed New Creature of JAH. Never shaving InI heads, neither allowing InI Locks to grow long and unelevated, but InI will Poll InI Heads, InI Heights, InI Truth. InI Locks will develop the manifestation of Coalesce Wisdom. InI will possess the core truth, and elevation of the Spiritual Mystical; the Iver Advancement not hue-manly possible. The Inner Court is InI Domain, beyond I Self.

    In teaching, it will be a Revelation that has to be experienced, not just knowledge. The difference between the Holy and profane are Spiritual Mystical Inner Revelations, very "Soul Stirring". Becoming Discerners between the unclean and the clean will require the Knowledge, of the sciences, of this world to perceive. The People chosen will be required to unshackle their "Heart Mind".

    In controversy, InI stand in Judgement. Overstanding the recesses in the depths of Truth. In judging, InI will pierce into the Judgement of JAH H.I.M.'s Law and statutes as they stand for Iternity, not in proximity or temporally. In "All Assemblies" InI Hallow (Holy Days, Days of Rest, Fasts, Consecrated Times,

Rastafari Livity

Rituals, Regimens, Vows, Prayers, etc.), and Every Sabbath InI continue to assist elevation.

InI come at no dead persons. It is only for the direct family and relations that InI come into contact with. An elevation and revelation must be present in them. This will be the type and kind, for all others belong and have their Priest. But InI must continue to become highly cleansed afterward, and be reckoned unto H.I.M. Seven days. This Is InI perpetual duty of Spiritual Mystical Empyreal Livity.

InI goeth into the unceasing sanctuary, the Iver Inner Court, Ministering Always, offering InI sin offering of the knowledge of this world. It is InI inheritance, JAH H.I.M. is InI Inheritance, InI Possession, Iver retained in InI Heart Mind and Mind's Heart. InI eat the meat offering, abled beyond the milk of this world, consuming what also is offered in sin offering, the trespass offering, and every dedicated thing in and of Israel: Contending for JAH; Striving for JAH; Rulership with JAH, Dominion with JAH.

Life exists to InI as the "Keepers of JAH's Light". H.I.M.'s First Fruits are the "Heights Revealed" of all things. Their deepest meaning, farthest application, and highest moral value become Knowledge and Wisdom to InI. Every oblation, of every sort of oblations, religions, spiritualities, ways of life, belief systems, and ideologies, that exist within InI Inner Sanctuary, are known, practiced, and Overstood by InI; that InI may stand in their Assemblies. No-Thing is Foreign to InI or beyond InI grasp and comprehension. InI bring the Blessings that come to rest in INI House.

The Priest may be known but is more likely unknown. There is a distance and magnetism emitted by him, and his responses can be elevating, confusing, empirical, obscured, brilliant, simple, scientific, or even philosophical, allegorical, or parable, but always serendipitous. That is the Grace that man needs to recognize concerning and involving Rastafari's Nazarite Vow.

The Locks

InI Locks possess and provide InI with an inherent power and ability that InI can, and should use. Any of the powers or capacities innate by InI brain or mind can be extended and amplified to higher levels, dimensions, and realms,

through InI Locks. This attribution gives InI necessary subjective and subconscious, sixth sense and third eye, initiation and operation; opening the intrinsic and intricate designs of Life, Livity, steps of righteousness and righteous behavior, speech, and moral direction. The highest potentials that are latent in InI pre-Locks state are many and immense. Those potentials become exceedingly applicable the more InI become studious. The processes of InI Locks are capable of functioning under varying environmental conditions, which allows adaptability and elevation.

InI Locks activate a cogitating of all things. Observers can note how InI elevate to take careful thought, and think carefully, about Life questions posed. This whole world is cogent for InI, appealing to InI intellect, powers of reasoning, and INI convincing abilities. Initially InI only possess a basic or reduced cognition compared to the Heights and vastness that InI can attain as InI Locks lengthen.

InI Locks are enmeshed in the ether, electromagnetic, earth's magnetic, and man's morphic fields. They absorb the light and energy information, and generate InI self-light and energy force. They transmit InI self-energy, force, and light into the Iniverse (Connecting to the electromagnetic spectrum, from gamma rays, x-rays, ultraviolet rays, and visible light, to the infrared, microwaves, and radio waves).

InI Locks are the foremost set of appendages InI possess in reception or transmission of higher and sublime information. InI carry out various forms of communications with their presence and types. InI Locks can transmit and receive the radiation of information, through electromagnetic waves within space-time. InI have an innate microcosmic programming signal of InI positional notation that is unique to InI only. It is the reason for InI "Relativity" of this world, it confirms InI "Karma" and experiences. It mobilizes InI Lessons and teaching so that InI receive InI Heights. InI obtain I signals by self-determining INI frequency and programing the waves of electromagnetic information radiation that saturates InI Iniverse, that is purposeful for InI. What InI obtain by programming is then transposed into InI construct of Reality, or in other words, interpreted into InI Livity, and is shared as a part of a collective macrocosmic totality.

Rastafari Livity

    These are the functions that are initiated and then expanded with the Nazarite Vow. It is a different state, it takes InI to a different place of observance. The mystery language, signs and symbols, and rituals, are all received from the Divine Light through InI Locks. Sustenance comes forth and maintains InI Life. The Divine Light Elevates, Inclines, and Informs of all the creation karmas descending upon InI. It is a status of Supreme Equality, given to man for his efforts, above the other created beings.

Rastafari Livity

Chapter Six

Anointing & Oils

...And thou shall make it an oil of Holy Ointment, an ointment compound after the art of apothecary: it shall Be a Holy Oil.

Anointing is a sacred duty that requires one to make the oil for anointing holy. This is a prayer and chanting ritual that calls on the Most High Jah to infuse His Mercy, Love and Protection into the oil that is to be consecrated. When this is done it doubles the covering that is given when the actual anointing takes place. The Blessings associated with anointing, in Rastafari, makes INI Hearts the "Sanctum Sanctorum" of the Most High Jah Rastafari, H.I.M. Haile Selassie 1st, Almighty I.

The Hebrews bring INI two different words for anoint. One "suk" related to the normal rubbing of the body with oil. The other "mashah", was employed primarily with reference to the act by which a person or thing was consecrated; by the pouring or smearing of the sacred oil. The latter type of anointing, in Rastafari, is a special act setting aside the anointed for divine service. Anointment not only sets aside and consecrates the person & object, but it also transfers elevation and solemnity to the recipient; and a portion of the Holiness and Strength of Jah Rastafari that He Gives to INI for such Worship.

Rastafari Livity

This is a Most Holy Duty with a Most Holy Oil, and should not be used as a perfume; which becomes a desecration of the oil used, but not of that which remains in the container; if it has been blessed with prayers and chanting. Also, the amount used should coincide with the Righteous Livity of the One being anointed. Everyone should be disciplined in the use of INI Holy Prayer Oil and the Anointing of it on INI.

BOOK OF SAMUEL:

"… There remaineth yet the youngest, and, behold, he keepeth the sheep…" Now he was ruddy and withal of a beautiful countenance, and goodly to look to. And Jah said, "Arise, anoint him: for this is he". Then Samuel took the horn of oil, and anointed him in the midst of his brethren: and the Spirit of Jah came upon David from that day forward.

"Therefore, will I give thanks unto thee, O Jah, among the heathen, and sing praises unto thy name. Great deliverance giveth He to His King; and showeth mercy to His anointed, to David, and to his seed for-Ivermore".

BOOK OF KINGS:

"…And let Zadok the Priest and Nathan the Prophet anoint Him (Solomon) there King over Israel: and blow ye with thee trumpet, and say, God save King Solomon"… So Zadok the Priest, and Nathan the Prophet, and Benaiah the son of Jehoiada, and the Cherethites, and the Pelethites, went down, and caused Solomon to ride upon King David's mule, and brought him to Gihon. And Zadok the Priest took a horn of oil out of the tabernacle, and anointed Solomon. And they blew the trumpet…

KEBRA NEGAST:

And they made ready the ointment of the "Oil of Kingship", and sounds of the large horn, and the small horn, and the flute and the pipes, and the harp and the drum filled the air, and the city resounded with cries of joy and gladness. And they brought the young man into the Holy of Holies, and he laid hold upon the horns of the altar, and sovereignty was given unto him by the mouth of Zadok the Priest, and by the mouth of Joas (Benaiah) the Priest, the commander of the army of King Solomon, and he anointed him with the "Holy Oil" of the ointment of Kingship. And he went out from the house of the Lord, and they called his name David, for the name of a King came to him by Law. And they

Rastafari Livity

made him to ride upon the mule of King Solomon, and they led him round about the city, and said, "We have appointed thee from this moment"; and then they cried out to him, "Bah (Long) live the royal father" … "It is meet and right that thy dominion of Ethiopia shall be from the River of Egypt to the West of the sun (i.e. To the setting of the son); blessed be thy seed upon the earth…" And again, his father (King Solomon) blessed him and said unto him, "The blessings of heaven and earth shall be thy blessings", and all the congregation of Israel said, "Amen". And his father (King Solomon) also said unto Zadok the Priest, "Make him to know and tell him concerning the judgement and decree of God which he shall observe there" (in Ethiopia)- as Menelik I, or Walda Tabbib (son of the wise man), or Ebna Hakim, Bayna-Lehkem, Ibn al-Hakim (in Arabic), "the son of the wise man" (these are the semetic Ge'ez, Amharic, and Arabic names of King Solomon's first born son, whom he called "David", after his father, upon his coronation).

H.I.M. ANOINTING:

"Preceded by waving incense burners… Following ancient customs, as when Samuel anointed David, and Zadok and Nathan anointed Solomon, so His Holiness, Abuna Qerillos, Archbishop of the Ethiopian Orthodox Tewahedo Church, anointed His Imperial Majesty, Haile Selassie I, on the Head, brow, and shoulders with seven differently scented oils and ointments of ancient prescription… finally, anointing H.I.M.'s Head with oil, the Abuna places upon H.I.M. the "Triple Crown". The Archbishop concludes the regal anointing with the words; "That, by the grace and the blessings which we have given, you may have an unshaken faith and a pure heart, in order that you may inherit the "Crown Eternal". So be it."

Here, InI have given Arat, daleth, or tetrad examples of "anointing" at its highest manifestations. The "Anointing" of Kingship is that of the Greatest Honor of Man. In ancient times, and up to the contemporary, Kingship was a title of authority. It gave the possessor the position of rulership, judgment and sometimes tyranny. But now InI have received the Heights of what "Kingship" Truly and Completely is. Now InI know that Kingship is a divine duty for man on earth; a consecration, an offering, a sacrifice, a burial, a resurrection, a communion with Jah. It is the result of repentance, the result of atonement, the

elevation of state that allows One into the "Holy of Holies". And all of this is gained through the "Anointing"!

The Holy Scriptures have over 1,035 verses referring to the subject and/or topic of "anointing", and its supporting elements and components. This act was well known as a religious and medicinal practice; very important in maintaining wellness and physical health; and for the enhancement of spiritual states, worship, prayer, and purification; according to records dating back to 4500 B.C. These writings, on papyrus, reveal medicinal formulas, the blending of aromatic substances for rituals, perfume recipes, blending of oils, and hundreds of oil recipes. Within these writings are descriptions of scented barks, resins of spices, and aromatic vinegar and liquids, used in rituals, temples, and embalming. Thus, oils, ointments, aromatics, savors, fragrances, incenses, etc., are definitively a part of the Heights of levels across the full spectrum of any Way of Life, society, belief system, religion, observance, tradition, etc.

In Rastafari Heights, Jah is definitively a lover of sweet-smelling savors and fragrances. The Fire of InI continuously burns away the wicked and unrighteousness, and leaves in its wake the ashes of purgation and re-birth; emitting a sweet-smelling savor of the empyrean, and the supernal fragrance of purity, consecration, and the sacred. Prayers, Chants, Praises are all sweet-smelling savors to the Most High JAH RASTAFARI, and the anointing with oils elevates them all for reception.

The act of "Anointing" has many operations, like: consecration, dedication, and a setting apart for a special purpose in JAH's Kingdom. Houses, Structures, articles of worship, clothing, and people should be anointed as a sign of separation to JAH.

As the Priest of the Home, husbands are encouraged to anoint their wives and children, for consecration, protection, and peace. Also, the Priest Husband anoints as a preparation for bible study, meditation, devotional time, fasting, praise, and worship. Anointing should also be done in times of sickness, fear, anxiety, oppression of the enemy, and defense.

The Bible dictionary mentions only two types of anointing: with oil or the Holy Spirit. In that, anointing with oil or Holy spirit are much more integrally related than most people realize, which explains why Bible translators sometimes use the anointing of oil or Holy Spirit interchangeably as synonymous

Rastafari Livity

verbs. As for the Holy Spirit, it can only be described as an overwhelming feeling, or sensation, of the rightness of thinking, feeling, and knowing in its anointing.

Both, the ancient Hebrew form of Messiah and the ancient Greek form of Christ literally means "anointed". To Be like it, as an inheritor or new creature, it would require one to know it. Therefore, in Rastafari, there is the "Anointing with Oils".

In Rastafari InI is separated, is consecrated, is the remnant of the righteousness of JAH's People. InI am elevated from the "Priesthood of Aaron" that are gone away, when Israel went astray, which went astray from JAH after their idols, to the "Priesthood of Zadok", the Levites and sons of Zadok; beginning with Azarius, who came to Ethiopia with Menelik 1, as his High Priest, that kept the charge of JAH's sanctuary when the children of Israel went astray from JAH. InI am the only ones that shall come near to JAH, to minister unto H.I.M., and to stand before H.I.M., to offer the fat and the blood (anointing). InI shall enter into H.I.M.'s sanctuary, and shall come near to JAH's Table, and will keep H.I.M.'s charge.

In the Nazarite Vow, within the Priest and Prophethood of Rastafari, no animal or blood sacrifice is made, but the Laws that govern offerings and sacrifice are still intact and mandated. JAH has said that H.I.M. will put H.I.M.'s Laws into InI mind, and write them in InI hearts, and H.I.M. will be to InI JAH, and InI shall be to H.I.M. a people.

There are over six hundred laws that govern JAH's people, Rastafari. These Laws govern the social religious behaviors of the people, and they transcend to the heavens for measure and weight. The offerings and sacrifices included within these laws, and the supporting sacrifices included within these laws, are the supporting elements and mechanics of submission and completion. They assist the Righteous in the Duty of Righteousness. They Compel the one to Unite his will with JAH's Will. They Elevate the Heights of Overstanding. They deepen the Truth of the teachings.

But now, in these Higher Heights, InI must extend the preservation of Life to all of creation. For in InI Edenic State of Aquarius, InI have no more need for InI brother animals to bear InI sacrificial burdens. InI sacrifice InI Selves Daily, and have become the Sacrament of the Most High JAH RASTAFARI, Haile Selassie 1st, Almighty I.

 *Rastafari Livity*

As is stated in the Holy Scriptures, in the book of Micha 4:3-5: "And He shall judge among many people, and rebuke strong nations afar off; and they shall beat their swords into plow shares, and their spears into pruning hooks: nation shall not lift up a sword against nation, neither shall they learn war any more. But they shall sit every man under his vine and under his fig tree; and none shall make them afraid: for the mouth of JAH of Host hath spoken it. For all people will walk everyone in the name of "his god", and InI will walk in the name of JAH RASTAFARI For-Iver and Iver".

In that day, saith JAH, will I Issemble her that halteth (limp), and I will gather her that is driven out, and her that is afflicted; And I will make her that halteth (limped) a remnant, and her that was cast far off a strong nation: and the Lord, JAH RASTAFARI, shall reign over them in Mount Zion from hence forth, even For-Iver.

To anoint is to announce INI offerings and sacrifices to JAH. It is to acknowledge the initiating and conclusion of prayer, chant, meditation, contemplation, praises, etc. It is to connect to the Iver-Living spirit of JAH. InI know that anointing is important to JAH because the words anoint, anointed, and anointing appears in more than 150 Spirit-inspired verses; placing it in a position of Ritual Primacy.

In these days and times, Rastafari is the "Primogeniture" of Righteousness and Holiness and is therefore consecrated, by Law, unto JAH. This consecration has to be fulfilled by the pouring and smearing that is done by anointing.

The Regal manifestation of Rastafari requires the senses to behold the "Regency" of InI with all faculties within InI family, house, and interactions. InI am seen, InI am heard, and InI am felt, but the perception of InI through the olfactory system was lacking. Now, with the Higher Heights of InI Mystical Coronation, InI olfaction sense needs to stand at attention upon Rastafari's arrival, and linger after InI departure. This is the fluorescent image that Rastafari leaves in the Heart-Minds of the people in anointing InI Selves.

Rastafari has perceived the fallacy in worship, praise, devotion, and religion nowadays. The People have forgotten, and are forgetting their

Rastafari Livity

"Blessedness". The reminders of salvation and elevation have passed into "oblivion". So now, more than ever, there needs to be a watchman, watchmen. There needs to be the "Pillar of Fire" by night for darkness has encompassed the minds and hearts of this world. Such as sitting in darkness and in the shadow of death, being bound in affliction and iron; because they rebelled against the "Words of JAH", and condemned the "Counsel of The Most High".

Anointing is the "weaponry" most effective against the darkness of this world. There is an immediate recognition of one being "not of this world" in the perception of prayer oils and ointments, by any congregation. It triggers a questioning. It activates an investigation. It initiates introspection.

Anointing troubles the negative spirits, demons, principalities and powers, and any spiritual wickedness in high places. The frowns on faces and unsettling of comfort and complacency are true indicators of what's in those who are in proximity. That "Legion Spirit" can't help but reveal Itself at the demand of the anointed presence, even unknowingly. The anointed comes thither to torment "Legion" before "the time" (it is a warning). Therefore, it is imperative that Rastafari anoints InI Self with regularity and often times.

The "Crown" is the most Important to anoint. It is why InI are Ras (head) Tafari (one to be feared). InI Locks, or headtop, is consecrated as a "Crown" upon anointing. InI anointing provides an amplification of Spiritual and Mystical Heights. InI anointing allows InI to withstand the insatiable gorging of wickedness and unrighteousness upon Righteous Light, Righteous Life, and Righteousness' Energies, as they enter and exit InI Being and Apex.

After InI anoint InI Head, brow, and shoulders, InI hands and feet should also become anointed. These are InI extremities that constantly interact with the energies of this world, and therefore need protection from its electromagnetic infectivity of current flow change, alternating currents, and alternative energies. This anointing is JAH going before them by day in a pillar of a cloud, to lead them the way… JAH took not away the pillar of the cloud by day… from before the people. And JAH came down in the pillar of the cloud, and stood in the door of the tabernacle (the Heart's Mind).

Chapter Seven

Houses and Mansions

Many of Rastafari use the scripture, "For as we have many members in one body, and all members have not the same office", or "For as the body is one and hath many members, and all the members of that one body, being many, are one body", as a teaching and/or explanation for the variances in the Rastafari collectives. Rastafari also uses, "In my Father's house are many mansions", as if it was for this reason and authority to create Rastafari Houses and Mansions. But is this bettering Rastafari? Does it have Rastafari moving as one body? Can Rastafari go to that place as One? The answer to these questions remains to be seen. Right now, I man want to express what should, foundationally, be happening in Rastafari as a product of the many mansions ideology.

Now, since it has been said that "science is religion's definition", I man will expound on this subject within Rastafari Knowledge, Wisdom, and Overstanding.

The mansions that are being spoken of in these verses are described as "abodes". An abode is defined as a dwelling place, a home, or a sojourn, which generally means "a waiting place"; especially when applied to the terrestrial. So,

Rastafari Livity

is Rastafari Houses and Mansions a waiting place? Is there something temporary about them? Or are they "Outgrowths" that will continue growing?

Rastafari Houses and Mansions are derivatives of Rastafari. In mathematics, one of the definitions of a derivative is "the slope of a curve at a given point". The concern here is what is the ascent or descent, and the rate, at which an ordinate of a point changes with respect to a change in the abscissa? In other words, are Houses and Mansions positive changes from the balancing and harmonic progression of the origin of Rastafari, or negative changes creating imbalance, division, confusion, chaos?

Rastafari, extending from Ethiopia, whom has stretched forth her hand unto JAH, is the "Illuminant" for the waning of Pisces and the ascension of Aquarius. It is the "Water Bearer", the Possessor of Livity, Producer of the Life Force, the Aperture and Gateway out of the Darkness of Babylon. This is what the Houses and Mansions are supposed to create in InI, and the whole of the world. This should be the duty and obligation of any House or Mansion's tenets as they are constructed for InI.

Lay A Foundation

Be careful, O children of JAH, that InI do what leads Rastafari to the obedience to JAH. No-thing should possess InI to fight against the will of JAH, unless he shall be counted among the worldly-minded rebels. Tenets must avoid injustice and the ambition to take the greater share. An example of a tenet is: Do not add beauty to the beauty given to InI by JAH at birth. Do not spoil the beard by shaving part of it, nor shall any man change his external appearance from its natural appearance; the law forbids all this. These two examples keep the mind from vanity.

If economically one is well, and do not need to have a craft for Rastafari Livity, still InI must not be without skills. When out from the home, stay with InI faithful and talk with them about the Spiritual Life. One must avoid enmity between any and quickly move beyond the lacking of any brethren. It is not for InI to judge, only to enlighten. Any who are asked to judge between brethren must do good always. By doing so JAH will grant INI great and incalculable honor. If it happens that Babylon creates anger with thee and another, do not let the

Rastafari Livity

sun set on thy anger. King Solomon has said: "The soul of those who bear malice will find death".

Ever since time immortal, Jah has called "His Remnant" to penance through the just, the prophets, and priests. JAH has taught through Abel, Seth, Enos, and Enoch. Through Noah, He called to those who lived before the flood, and through Lot, who gave hospitality to strangers, Jah called out any who lived rightly in Sodom. After the "Deluge", JAH called Melchizedek, Abraham, and Job, with those who could both hear and see. In Moses, JAH called the Egyptians, children of Israel, and that mixed multitude, that Moses, Aaron, Joshua, the son of Nun, Caleb and Phineas brought forth from captivity; spiritually, mentally, and physically. JAH Himself has come to share with His Remnant, manifesting the True Power of His Kingdom, Being Within. But when a man works night and day in this transitory time, neglecting what concerns Iternity, and when he troubles himself about food that perishes and goes to ruin, despising what is infinite, how can he avoid being told: "The heathens are more just than you", or just as JAH bitterly reproached Jerusalem, saying: "Sodom is more just than thee"? The skill of Rastafari consists in Spiritual Wisdom that manifest, and InI occupation is the Worshiping and Praising of JAH. Rastafari must forward with Spiritual Strength in order to be Wise, Masterful, and Sagacious. Rastafari nascented to be devoted to working in JAH's Service; "For InI Labor not for the food which perishes, but for the food which is for the Life Everlasting".

Rastafari must never be idle, nor should InI reveal the mysteries without initiation; "Do not cast InI pearls before swine". And when infidels hear Rastafari talking about His Imperial Majesty, Haile Selassie I, because they lack knowledge of faith in prophesy being fulfilled, they scoff at Rastafari, and it seems to them a lie, but it is written: "Woe to him because of whom My Name is blasphemed among the Gentiles". Whosoever curses unjustly, curses himself. Rastafari teaches to accept what JAH has sent InI with gratitude and fear.

Therefore, Rastafari's groundation begins with self-initiated corrections:

- Do not speak ill against any man, nor plot to do him evil.
- Do not be double-hearted or double-tongued or greedy, wanting the greater share.
- Do not give bad advice.
- Do not be envious, do not scoff at others, and do not be given to killing, nor easy to anger, for anger leads to killing.

Rastafari Livity

- Do not be lustful, for lust leads to fornication; and when the Satan of anger unites with the Satan of lustfulness they ruin whosoever receives them.
- Do not entertain the dwelling of an evil spirit, it is a wound to the soul. If the Satan finds a little entrance, he widens the entrance and brings all the evil spirits and introduces them into the soul. A man so wounded cannot in any way arise and see the Truth.
- Do not be a liar, nor lover of money, or of vain praise, for all these lead to stealing.
- Do not grumble, because grumbling leads to blasphemy.
- Do not become haughty, but love and be the companion of just and humble persons.

These are inner convictions to the betterment of the man who is to perform His Spiritual Duties. InI must have a Self-Elevating duty as a Foundation to the continued Elevation towards the Mystical Revelation. Eldership is very unique in Rastafari, and is determined upon by many factors of one's Livity. It is why a neophyte shall not be a priest until he is learned and until the sanctity of his life, the firmness of his faith, and the purity of Rastafari, from his teachings, are proved. Lest he be puffed up with pride and fall into judgement of the Satan.

The fear of JAH is a good thing. A man must not be an Elder who has no fear of JAH RASTAFARI, His Imperial Majesty, Haile Selassie I, King of Kings, Lord of Lords, Conquering Lion of the Tribe of Judah, and is not prudent in this. This Fear is a Fear of self-conviction, self-judgement, self-analysis, and introspection. Not of what one may Fail to do for JAH, for JAH has no such need of these, but of what one may fail to do "towards" JAH of his own choosing. For many persons have delivered themselves into the fetters of a Dreadlocks type life, so much so that they wasted themselves away with patois and persisted in "Impostor-fari", doing nothing to make others grow up before JAH, and that they persevered in fulfilling only the minor precepts of Rastafari. Yet when their locks lengthen, and they appeared like priests and had to bring others back, to the right way, none of them could do it. So they lost the sanctity they previously gained and were ruined irremediably. Therefore, Eldership shall not be admitted simply because one grows old on the middle rank, but he shall be so admitted only if he is deemed worthy.

Rastafari Livity

In Rastafari is the accumulation of what is called clergy; priest, bishop, deacon, archbishop, archdeacon, and minister. Rastafari, in the full capacity of Houses and Mansions, is the teacher, the one who instructs the people and others. InI is the leader in prayer and is responsible for every duty pertaining to the House and Mansion of JAH RASTAFARI, and is superior as the lector after prayer times.

The Kings who lived in the time of the Old Testament kept their armies but abandoned war; they sought peace in order to save the body. But now Rastafari have received the Priesthood from JAH to save the body and the soul from perdition. So as the soul is superior to the body, so also Priesthood is superior, in honor, to Kingship. It punishes whosoever deserves punishment and forgives whosoever deserves forgiveness. And if he who rises against the King deserves punishment, even if he is son or friend, how much more deserving of punishment is he who opposes Jah's Priests? So as Priesthood is superior to Kingship, the punishment of one who opposes Jah's Priests is greater than the punishment of one who opposes the King, and neither one shall escape punishment.

As an ethicist, Rastafari teaches that every man shall abide in his rank, and no one of InI shall attempt to take another's position by violence. If any do so, they will call the wrath of JAH upon themselves, as did the sons of Aaron, Nadab, and Abihu when they usurped the priestly position against the command of JAH. Moses, to whom JAH spoke, fixed the foundational requirements for the ordination of Priest. He has stated who, according to these requirements, will be priests, and has duly explained everything. He has set out what is forthcoming to the Levites on account of their rank. For Rastafari, this is continued through the Kingship of King David and King Solomon, Empress Makeda, Emperor Menelik, Ezekiel 44, and His Imperial Majesty, Haile Selassie I.

If there were not a law and prescribed distinctions between each degree, and every other, every new creature would serve with only one name (purpose). But when InI Elders learned from JAH, the order of various duties, the Houses and Mansions came forth; allowing Rastafari to maintain rank and abide in Truth and duty. No House or Mansion of Rastafari exists in error. All are portions of the gates of the Holy City coming down from JAH. So that the tabernacle of JAH is

Rastafari Livity

with InI, and He will dwell with InI. And Rastafari shall be His people, and JAH Himself shall be with Rastafari and be InI's Christ in Kingly Character. For as it is written: "I will give unto him that is a thirst of the fountain of the Water of Life Freely; this is Aquarian Time. He that overcometh shall inherit all things; and I will be his God, and he shall be My son".

Chapter Eight

The Hebraic Element

As InI know, H.I.M. is a descendent of King David, through King Solomon, from Emperor Menelik I. This entire lineage is of Hebraic quality. It is Hebraic Blood, Hebraic Heritage, Hebraic Traditions, and Hebraic Culture; that is in H.I.M. Haile Selassie I. None of this can be taken away, or excluded, merely from the fact of observation that H.I.M.'s Orthodoxy in Christianity became established. H.I.M.'s Orthodoxy is an extension of what His lineage, heritage, and culture had previously brought to Him.

According to His lineage, H.I.M. is of the Hebraic Genius, being descendent of His Great Elder Eber, biologically. H.I.M. is also of the Yisraelite Genius; being a designate of the Tribe of Yehuda, whom Yacob, Yisrael, gave true and divine authority of rulership. This culminates into H.I.M. being a Hebrew-Yisraelite by simple birthright, needing no further proof necessary for Rastafari to adhere to the beckoning and announcement of this as InI's actuality.

Rastafari Livity

This birthright allows for H.I.M. Haile Selassie I to assimilate Christianity's Orthodoxy in order to continue the messianic principle that Divine Evolution necessitates in monotheism. But, it is InI who must be instructed and instruct Rastafari to acknowledge the Divine Harmony that exists in this Union. H.I.M. is InI's example of the reality of being completely monophysitic. Not having the Hebraic Element present is rendering prophecy null and void, it's rendering H.I.M. Haile Selassie I non-authoritative, and it is rendering Rastafari just Christian like, in which none of these above is InI's Truth.

In H.I.M. exist the homoiousia and homophoyly of Hebrew Yisraelite and Ethiopian Orthodox Christianity, and in no way, shape, measure, calculation, or form can either be separated from the other. H.I.M.'s birthright and culture created this homogeneity by Divine Instruction. (Psalms 18:50)

Now what is the core, the root, the essence of Rastafari? What InI do know is that its general fullness is in the embodiment of His Imperial Majesty Haile Selassie I, and the completeness, the prophecy being fulfilled, is a nascent, or a catapult, in our times, to assemble and correct the path that man has taken as true, but is not. In order to realize this fact, Ras Tafari, H.I.M. Haile Selassie's I essential nature will be anatomized and critically analyzed, so that the legacy of the evolution from King Solomon of Yisrael, to Menelik I of Ethiopia, to H.I.M. Haile Selassie I of Ethiopia, through the aeons before and towards the aeons of the future, remains prosperous to the practitioners of the knowledge and wisdom that comes from this Subjective Royalty of the Divine; and not become calcified and pernicious by not mandating contemporary enlightenment upon the ill state of spiritual reality in this world.

In order to begin any anatomizing, or analyzing, the components and elements, have need of identification; so that they may now contribute to the Overstanding of what Rastafari has; that is being significantly reduced by being underlooked. The multiple components that InI will search out, which are truly one and the same, and expound on, are the Ethiopian Spiritual and Cultural Elements. For it is this union that most everyone avoids or aren't aware of; allowing them to perform under their own ideas, even though it is staring InI, so obviously, right in the face.

Rastafari Livity

But first, let's take a look at the common ground of ancestry that all Rastafari originates from.

It is the Prophet's, Marcus Garvey, Black-to-Afrika Movement that culminated into Rastafari. What is said is that "InI teachings affirm that InI have found a new ideal. Whilst InI God has no color, yet it is human to see everything through one's own spectacles. InI believe in the God of Ethiopia, the Everlasting God, God the Son, God the Holy Spirit, the One God of All Ages. That is the God in whom InI believe, but InI shall worship Him through the spectacles of Ethiopia".

So InI journey begins.

The God of Ethiopia is a farther reaching ideal than anyone has previously supposed. You see, spirituality permeates the Ethiopian's Life, so a concept like divinity is not able to be boxed up, neatly wrapped and given as a gift. It is a truly living entity that affects and is the effect; especially when InI search out all of the minutias of the Ethiopian Spirituality. It is why, over the Ages, Ethiopia has continued to be a major center to the beliefs and practices of the world. InI God is Iternal and Infinite.

Ethiopia's Ancestry in spiritual, mystical, matters extend as far back as spiritual concerns are documented. InI's connection to JAH, and how He reveals Himself, through time and the ages, give InI a unique quality of adaptation and assimilation. This uniqueness gives the Ethiopian the ability to be all that JAH requires InI to be. Everything commanded has its place in the Ethiopian's Life.

Rastafari adheres to the entire and complete Ethiopian Spirituality, its inspiratories and their messages of total attentiveness and submission to JAH in InI Lives. If InI can use the proper names of the Scriptures, it can be said that Rastafari is engineered towards coalescing the Orit (Torah, Old Testament), Gospels, and Epistles (New Testament) into the true "Marriage of the Lamb". Rastafari is where the Ancient Judeo-Ethiopic and Antiquitous Orthodox Order are excellently tantamount.

Rastafari Livity

Yeshua, being a descendant of King David, through King Solomon, from King Rehoboam, gave the instructions as to how InI should live in a time that is now distant from that of InI's ancestry. It was complete with biblical implications from InI's interactions with the oppressors and enemies of God's People, while keeping the commandments as they were given to InI forefathers. In this, there are variations but never change. "Greater things than these will ye do" gives InI the capability to use advancements in knowledge to continually proceed in that righteous Hebraic manner; rather than fail to be aware of the applicable nature of InI Hebraic Lineage, and just change everything and call it a new religion or belief.

So what's "New"? InI Father says that there is "Nothing New," so why has InI not approached this illusion of "New Belief" and anatomized it, discovering what it really and truly is? A complacent, divisive, separatist, and conquestian doctrine isn't of the harmonious nature of the Divine, yes, none of that is, and probably so much more. InI, as a people, are the greatest of assimilators, but now all InI do is simulate. InI no longer incorporate, InI now partially partake. Bringing harm and injury to the entire world by not taking InI "Rightful Place".

The proof of lineage required, the act of coronating, the permeation of spirituality in daily life, and unavoidably, the possession of the Ark of the Covenant, are all the impossible facts present, in proving the Hebraic Elements of Ethiopia, that necessarily need recognition in Rastafari. The Gospel of the Kebra Negast is insurmountable evidence of InI Hebraic Quality. InI Beta Israel Ancestry, that lives today, is undoubting clarity. The Semitic Origin and designation of InI's Ge'ez and Amhareena Alphabet, and Language, cannot be even slightly disproved. All of this is telling Rastafari, announcing to the world, that these elements must be put into operation before any true growth, development, or advancement, can ever take place in Rastafari. For InI are Nazarites, separated unto God, and that is where the Hebraic is initiated.

Spiritual Awareness, quality of living, interactivity with nature, InI's Edenic perception of Life, and InI's overall theme of Love for all, is every bit as Hebraic as it is Orthodox Christianity. Yeshua taught His message from the Hebraic and Essenian View, which is derived from the Hebrew Israelite Judaic Branch. As far as Rastafari necessitates, the Wisdom of the Ethiopic Hebrew

Rastafari Livity

Culture, being viable for millennias, gives more value to InI than the Ashkenazic or Sephardic cultures of the Jewish. The difference in these is that the Ashkenazic and Sephardic cultures seem to only wish to be known as the partial Jews, rather than the full and complete Hebrew Yisraelites prior to captivity and before splintering into factions, after the Age of King Solomon; which Rastafari is now drawing itself back to through H.I.M.'s Hebraic Element.

To be associated with being Ethiopian is truly a high spirituality to possess. It means that InI seeks the pleasure of Spirituality towards the Mystical, and rendering any explanation of the Divine impossible to fully define, articulate, or comprehend, through the norms of the tangible manifested world. It places InI in the realm that commits InI to the Essential Nature, rather than the objective appearance, of the Iniverse. It transports InI to the super-consciousness of interconnectedness and entanglement in creation. It elevates InI to coadunation of the Divine and its spark within InI. In one word, it is Omniscient to be of Ethiopia.

Now here is the auspiciousness of the exclusivity of the Ethiopian Spiritual Awareness, "Expressive Abstraction". It isn't even remotely possible for a people to produce a simultaneously existing, intangible and tangible, Ultimate Divine Entity, with an inefficiency in neurotransmission and synapse function in the primary abstract region of the brain. The mental faculty that does this is only dominant in a Melanotic People, others lack the high degree of processability necessary to accept the abstraction as a reality. In other words, they do not have the ability to reach within their minds and bring forth that which will become, because it already is real, type of concepts.

The place where all of the previous factual observations become infinitely important is when InI considers the Divine Covenant with King David that the Most High made. King David was given the covenant of always having His seed on the throne. Now, because the current state of Yisrael is democratic, and the Most High's words are always Truth, InI must Overstand where and what is the kingdom of today. Once that is established, InI must seek to place one, of the seed of King David, on that throne. This can obviously only be done in one manner, and that is in the manner of the spiritual/mystical. This exegesis may not be acceptable to some, because of their wish to maintain the status quo, but

Rastafari Livity

Rastafari or not, there must be a realization of InI's current state of affairs as being insufficient and unfulfilling of scriptural facts.

Rastafari Decentralization has the merit of satisfying the needs of the environment that a Rastafari House happens to be in, but it must also allow for the fundamentals to be expressed uniformly in all of them. InI cannot have such drastic changes, from one House to the next, in the fundamental teachings. There has to be a primus, a first initial thing, a nascency because we do occupy existence in a manifested world. That first thing, the first instance of recognition by Rastafari, of His Imperial Majesty Haile Selassie I, is in no doubt the Divine Hebraic Element. For in His conception, this was in existence, within Him, while still in His Mother's Womb. His Orthodoxy, the baptismal tenets of Ethiopian Christianity, came much later.

This realization is in no way meant to exterminate the teachings and practices of the Ethiopian Orthodox Tewahedo Church. They are well worthy of their recognition, but they do not sufficiently satisfy the requirements of Rastafari in InI's duty and obligation. InI are spiritual leaders of a different nature than Christianity allows without the Hebraic Element. The King and Queen nature is aided by the Priest/Prophet characteristic in Rastafari. InI don't simply belong to the people in administering justice between them, InI are also ministers unto the Most High, exacting upon this world whatever it is that needs expression from H.I.M. This is not the familiar way that leadership is carried out Christianicly. Christianity has separated this role into two roles that do not, even minimally, communicate cohesively. That is why it is so difficult to get the necessary thoughts, behaviors, and actions of righteousness, treating neighbors as InI would like to be treated, into the hearts of the people, in order to produce that One Love that Rastafari demands.

So again, there needs to be this incorporation of the Hebraic Essentials into Rastafari as a fundamental truth, and teaching, that can enact upon InI's focal consciousness an elevation. Ethiopian Orthodox Christianity, Hebrew Yisraelite, and Rastafari have all waned in power and influence, and have now become novelties and footnotes to society's operations; instead of being the head they have become the tail. A lot of this is because of the separation of the Hebraic Element that is readily perceivable if anyone decided to look. The

actions and behaviors that are now taking place, as regular occurrences and events, show that the people have become inebriated; but InI must not also stand inebrious in the partiality that people possess that doesn't contain the full excellence of H.I.M. Haile Selassie I. To annul the expression of the slackness in duty and responsibility, InI must take hold of InI's World with Divine Qualities expected of the One's of H.I.M.

The question of why the Hebraic Element is necessary, especially with the advent of Yeshua and H.I.M Haile Selassie I, may still be present and requires a more detailed explanation for its position in Rastafari, that is not a problem. The Hebraic Element, that is being brought forth here, is that seat of existence of InI's spirituality. It is Hebrew, and it is derived from Eber. Eber is the germination or beckoning that signifies that an unfolding of the spirit is taking place. It is that which causes InI to pass on from InI's old concept of mortality, to begin to consider the reality of the eternal. The quickening that is spoken of in the scriptures is an actuality and derivative of Eber. It is in this igniting that InI go beyond the purely sensate, physical, earthly, manifested, objective form of thought. InI begin to know of a reality beyond flesh and bones because InI recognize the veil now. It is here that InI's feelings and sensations all become subjective. InI become serendipitous in Knowledge, Overstanding, and Wisdom. The purely material, in this world, begins to reveal more of its essential nature, as a reality. It is a passing over from the region of the physical man towards the mystical one.

Now, InI may still be somatopsychic, but this is the beginning of a conscious alliance with the Mind of Spirit. Not being mundane, but becoming Ultramundane. Not yet being celestial, but going beyond terrestrial. Elevating from the sensate recorders of the brain, and its analytical reasoning. The Superconsciousness is coming online, and it will activate the Inner Man, the astral, so that InI can begin to Truly Live. Yes, I said Live, because without this Hebraic Element InI is caught up in the flesh, where death is a sure reality. The Hebraic Element of Eber gives InI that which passes further, on the other side, then InI can accomplish without it. Having the Hebraic Element of Eber ignited is a prerequisite, and is imperative, to any full spiritual development.

Rastafari Livity

When InI measure the Hebraic Element of Eber, scripturally, InI become aware of the actuality of Eber being the last instance of man being coadunate. The several millenniums since then have produced a separation so vast that man is no longer one with even himself, let alone anyone else. And with man's, and that includes Rastafari, so-called advancements; in technology, medicine, and society, InI have been cast into a state of entropy that is ever increasing in its suppositional differentiation of Life. In other words, InI are shattering in darkness, and so, a return, an about-face, is in order for the redemption of InI. In Rastafari, that would be done with the acknowledgment of the Hebraic Element that already exist in InI because of Ras Tafari, H.I.M. Haile Selassie I.

This is InI's Truth. A remembrance must be made into the transition of InI self from a low to a high state. This Higher State is caused by the aforementioned Hebraic Element of Eber. But, InI owe true allegiance to the Spiritually being revealed to InI, through faith, which is found in only one place, based on InI's history, Abram, and in its fullness Abraham. Faith in the Invisible Forces is of Abram. Focusing that faith on the One God is of Abram. To intuitively know God Consciousness is of Abram. To possess the highest of ideals is of Abram. Abraham evolves from Abram being the Father of Heights, Father of Exaltation, to the source and founder of the multitudes who would accomplish this while still in the flesh; giving InI the ability of mind to make substance out of ideas. InI faith is the realization of the Power of the Invisible affecting the visible. Going from the unsure state of flesh to full communication with the Super Mind State, and not remaining somantical in any way. This, Abramic and Abrahamic Ideal of Faith, is the nexus in the Union between the Hebraic Element and Ethiopian Orthodox Christianity. This is the certitude of a complete righteousness within the wholeness of Rastafari, H.I.M. Haile Selassie I. To not formally exemplify and expound so would clearly render one delusional in True Spiritual Matters. The elaborately complex, but yet innocently simple, effect of this factuality created this necessary explanation of an elevational wisdom that was being denied; so that suffering and oppression, within Westernized Endemic Spirituality, could be treated and corrected.

 *Rastafari Livity*

There is no other cure for the calamities of this world except in the discovery of a perspicacious panacea that already exists within a system of awareness. That system, the one that InI ancestors originated, is a system of self-discovery. For INI Self, in this present moment, it is Rastafari. Rastafari has no limits, and is farther reaching than InI are practicing; in the applicable tenets of spirituality. "Head Creator" means that everything is for use in the righteous attainment of the spiritual, be it physically mundane or Mystical. But what has happened is that the religions, and their rituals, are being accepted as the excellence of practice, but surely aren't. The spiritual excellence that is sought after is subjective and incorporeal. The lessons to be learned are metaphysical and discarnate. InI must, I Selves, become asomatous, using only the faculty of the mind and spirit, intelligence and comprehension, inference and subtilization.

This explains why Rastafari can suffuse and be imbued with multiple disciplines of religion simultaneously without confusion. It is a search for the totality and completeness of InI Self, and not the want to satisfy tradition or what is considered empirical. Rastafari is Freedom, so InI can't be indoctrinated with anything that is contrary to Liberation; so know that exploration is beneficial. InI possess definite inalienable rights; from the Creator of the Heavens and Earths. While these cannot ever be limited, reduced, taken away, or expunged, they can be forgotten, transferred, lied about, misrepresented, corrupted, and removed far from InI's reach. It is why InI's search, discovery, record, and teaching, must continue to keep InI's Light lit. If InI sit idly by and let the powers of this world express their own ideas, and agenda, the injuries that are now a part of InI's daily lives will continue, and increase in their destruction of InI's Knowledge of Truth.

The Hebraic Element itself has been taken to be out of fashion, and some olden thing of the past. But what is forgotten about the Hebraic Element is that it is a permeating innate entity, full of vigor; so to remove it entirely, and still seek spirituality's fullness, is impossible. A limited knowledge of, or understanding in, can be just as harmful, over time. So Rastafari, being Timeless, requires that "something" that is Timeless itself. Rastafari needs to become an

Rastafari Livity

anchorite to this world, so that the world does not perish from the wickedness of its ways.

To begin in the fundamental teachings of Rastafari, with the incorporation of the Hebraic Element, InI start with the knowledge of a Creator of the Heavens and Earths that is Iver-Present and Iver-Knowing; without even the slightest Planck measure of fallacy in the existence of Him. Based on the Hebraic Element, coming from the Kebra Negast, JAH is, and within everything, without prejudice. This is the first, and only, example needed by Rastafari to stay in a singularity of mindset when it comes to Life in Spirit. This is what the current state of Rastafari must be measured up against. And since InI have done this, it has revealed that the standard isn't being met in Rastafari. InI are lacking a sense of importance and obligation.

Once the Perception of The Creator of the Heavens and Earths becomes omnipresent, omniscient, and omnipotent. He must now also be fully omnificent, omnifarious, omnigenous, and omnicompetent, with omnitude in purpose. In other words, that InI can only use after describing H.I.M.'s totality through the Omni prefix, because they themselves are inefficient in doing so alone, the Creator of the Heavens, and the Earths, must become and be Every and All things to InI. H.I.M. is never just a part or portion of anything, but the complete thing is of H.I.M. InI must Omnify Rastafari, H.I.M. Haile Selassie I.

Omnipresent: present in all places at all times.

Omniscient: having infinite awareness, understanding, and insight; knowing all things.

Omnipotent: Almighty or unlimited power: an agency or force of unlimited power and influence.

Omnificent: creating all that comes into existence; unlimited in creative power.

Omnifarious: all of varieties, forms, or kinds.

Omnigenous: composed of or containing all varieties.

Omnicompetent: having jurisdiction or legal capacity to act in all matters.

Omnitude: totally, universality.

Rastafari Livity

INTERLUDE

• •

Omnify

With the need to Omnify Rastafari comes also the need to identify a "Way" of doing so that can include the complexities the brain accepts, elevations the spirit requires, and Antiquitous Origin Truth demands. There is a Way that is known to InI of accomplishing all these within InI power and effort.

• •

This brings InI to the topic of a most omni system of thought, contemplation, and realization, "The Tree of Life." The Tree of Life System has known to InI, at this time, three variants that InI will summary describe to InI. First, there is the Kabbalic System, secondly the Kemetic System, and thirdly the Yorubic System. Now, this is not an order of their origin, importance, or usefulness. InI have just listed each in the way that allowed InI to state them. What's omni about the Tree of Life Systems are their myriad of layers explaining & assisting in the knowledge of the manifestation of Life into this materialized world. For example, starting with the Kabbalic System, there are four worlds to be known. The Four Worlds are the States of Existence, the Levels of Purity, the Hierarchies of Power that allow something to be. Each World brings with it the Substance and Sustenance of the previous World so that there may be a lineage, a foundation, of Strength and Power in it. It all begins in the Infinite Realm of Divinity, Divine Providence, or the Eternal State of JAH. As it devolves, that Eternal Nature is built upon allowing an eventual temporal manifestation to take place, and an experience of it to happen objectively.

Rastafari Livity

The Four Worlds have names that describe them, to a degree. The first is Atziluth, the Archetypal World, World of Emanations, or Divine World. This World is the Origin World and brings forth Being. The second is Briah, the World of Creating, also known as the Most Common Physical Limit of Overstanding among InI sages, prophets, gurus, and messengers. This is the World where the Eternal Voice speaks to the Highest State of Man. The third is Yetzirah, the World of Formation. This is the "Blue Print World." This is the World that explains what Creation should be. It is the World that will reveal to the Meditator or Contemplator where the Errors of Life exist, and what their corrections are. This is also where the Messages, Teachings, and Scripts all derive their languages. The fourth is Assiah, the World of Manifestation, Matter, and Actions. This is the World where it all goes down. Everything that happens here happens because InI am at the conclusion of the Devolution of Divinity, but at the same time in the Evolution of Objectivity. In other words, it is in Assiah that Spiritual Righteousness and Spiritual Wickedness Clash, Contrast, and Conflict with each other. Assiah is the "Battleground World" where Success or Failure is measured.

In each of these Four Worlds are nine Spheres of Influence that give elements, components, and structure to each World, and the objectification of a Principle Ideal. A Tenth Sphere is the finality of that Principle Ideal and, at the same time, the beginning of its furthered objectifying into the Next World. The Tenth Sphere is the Link and Lock of lineage.

Including the Spheres, there are Thirty-Two Paths, Levels, or Degrees of Intelligences, that all contribute to the Knowledge, Overstanding, and Wisdom of what is being contemplated. Each sphere has a name that describes what it gives or reveals about the Principle Ideal; at that particular point of reference. It is a very elaborate system that this writing doesn't allow to be fully expounded on at this time. In summary though, InI have Four Worlds, Forty Spheres, and One Hundred Twenty-Eight Paths, Levels, or Degrees, in the Kabbalic System, that reveals an Omniness of Perception that can be had when mastered.

In the Kemetic System, or in the name that InI knows this system better, The Meter Neter, there isn't a Four World System, to InI knowledge, but a One World System that describes manifestation from a Zero sphere to a Tenth Sphere. It teaches that a descent was made to manifestation, but that an ascension must be caused before descension becomes infinite in the Material World; which is the description or meaning of Hell. Ascension also must continue

when descension becomes the decease of the existence in the Material World, and existing in the Non-Material World becomes the State of Being.

In the Kemetic System, there is a myriad of needed principles taught throughout it. From the initiation into the system, to the non-material existence, there are rituals, practices, and memorizations that need to be acquired so that Omni-Perception can be gained and maintained.

The Kemetic System's Structure is for one who can benefit from its language, components, and elements that weave a construction of growth and elevation in their Life Manifested, and in the Living Beyond. InI development prior to initiation allows this system to be applicable, InI singularity is why. There needs to be certain Life Seeds planted that can be triggered by the beckoning of the Kemetic Tree.

InI each have an Indigenous Physical Origin, a Singularity. This origin is the Entangled Particle that is the key of the system's beckoning and the unlocking of its language, components, and elements, that initiate the growth and elevation of InI. InI fertileness is developed and nurtured, by experiences; preparing InI to welcome the spiritual cultivation soon to be gained by the system, in this case the Kemetic, of InI particular type.

The Ten Spheres in the Kemetic System are taught to be Man's Faculties of his Higher Original Being and his Lower Experiential Self. It teaches that the movement from lower to higher spheres is evolution, and that each sphere that is awakened, opened and known, is an evolution of man that allows his use of that faculty, hence bettering His Life. There are realms, levels, dimensions, categories, and degrees maintained by the unified working of a Multiplicity of Agencies. This is the Interdependence that the Kemetic System uses for Spiritual Maturation.

This is the second of three systems configured as a Tree of Life System, that aides in the development of the Unseen Realm in InI; the Realm of Eber. Eber, meaning passed over; come over; overcome; on the other side; beyond; region beyond; beyond the world; ultramundane, is the origin and root of the Hebraic Element. It is what the Tree of Life Systems all expound on, in their various ways, to bring InI to a conclusion and a Beginning in Living.

Rastafari Livity

At this point InI have rudimentarily summarized two Tree of Life Systems that explain that there is decent of divinity, and can possibly be an ascending back to divinity, of the physical; with diligent application of the Knowledge, Overstanding, and Wisdom dwelling beyond religion. One, the Kabbalic, uses a Four-World Complexity of Spiritual Development that is structured for a particular type and state. The other, the Kemetic, uses a Single-World Structure of Spiritual Cultivation that is designed for its particular type and state of physical mental being. Both system's effectiveness is largely dependent on the Life Seeds planted, and the degree of consciousness awakened at initiation. This will determine the level of Omni-Perception acquired and applicable in InI Life.

InI description of Yoruba, being a Tree of Life System, is only for the purpose of uniformity in expounding on the Omni-Perception gained, through the Awareness of Reward, within the Hebraic Element in Rastafari. InI have not been taught this directly, but has gained this Overstanding in the Iditations of JAH RASTAFARI; and His Imperial Majesty's Teaching that "All The Mystics Have Agreed." InI draw upon that Harmony in Life, and of Yoruba, to be applicable to InI's Livity. With that said, a concise description of InI Overstanding of Yoruba, as a Tree of Life System, is as follows.

In the Yorubic Tree of Life, Olodumare is the Complete Tree. Olodumare is the All of All, Matterical of Material, Subject, and Object. Olodumare completes the Full Spiritual Journey, Spiritual Cultivation, Spiritual Maturation, and Elevation. The Nine Spheres of the Yorubic Tree are named for the Orisha's, or deities, that Emanate the Attributes, Abilities, Knowledge and Wisdom of Olodumare for man's purpose. The Spheres, or Orishas, require practices, rituals and, more importantly, identification in order to be useful to the practitioner. It is taught that missing any aspect of proper practice, ritual, or identification can also bring about harm, which is the mystifying reason why most choose not to become knowledgeable of, and participants in, this particular Tree of Life System.

The component that makes the Tree of Life System of Yoruba an Advanced Version is the fact that one can gain his Highest State through one Orisha, one Sphere, and that Orisha's governance of their head. Meaning, in this system, there is a specific deity for each and every person in this Realm, and that deity assists that practitioner in their Spiritual Cultivation and Maturation. There are rituals and practices that need to be applied in order to receive this

Rastafari Livity

Guidance, and with those duties carried out, success is acquired. This is the most streamlined and direct Tree of Life System. It is concise, and, if a comparison can be made, would be the equivalent of the Briah World of the Kabbalic, or the Upper Five Spheres of the Kemetic. Its operation in the Material World is also of the most unconformable, uncanny, unique type, which again, grants an enigmatic and ethereal mystique.

    The Tree of Life Systems are assistors in the Attainment of Omni-Perception, Obtainable, within the Hebraic Element in Rastafari. Each one produces a Spiritual Ability that is built upon within InI Circadian Rhythm and catapults InI into an Enlightened Abstract Meditation that reveals Truth and Overstandings.

Rastafari Livity

THE FOUR TREES

Atziluth, the Boundless World of Divine Names – Yod (hand)

Briah, the Archangelic World of Creations Head – Intelligence, Knowledge – He (window)

Yetzriah, the Hierarchal World of Formations Chest -feelings, imaginations – Vau (nail)

Assiah, the Elemental World of Substances Belly – Manifestations – He (window)

Rastafari Livity

– Receptive Female   **+ Active Male**

1

Ausar/Keter
Pineal Gland
Crown Above
I AM Eheieh
Hayo+Ha Kodesh=Holy Living Ones
Primum Mobile
Omnipresent **(KMT)**

Covenant of Unity
⋯⋯
The Thought

3 ♄

Seker/Binah
Understanding North
God of Gods Yehovah Elohim
Thrones=Erelim
Saturn
Omnipotent **(KMT)**

2

Tehuti/Chokmah
Right Hemi
Wisdom East
Essence of Being Yehovah
Wheels=Ophanim
The Zodiac
Omniscent **(KMT)**

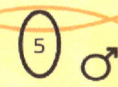
5 ♂

Herukhuti/Gevurah
Left Arm
Severity Evil
God the Potent Elohim Gibor
Burning Ones=Seraphim
Mars
Divine Justice **(KMT)**

6 ☉

Heru/Tepheret
Heart
Beauty Air
God the Strong Eloah Vaaath
Messengers=Malakhim
Sun
Will **(KMT)**

4 ♃

Maat/Chesed
Right Arm
Mercy Good
God the Creator El
Electric Ones=Hashmallim
Jupiter
Divine Law **KMT**

8 ☿

Sebek/Hod
Left Leg
Honor West
Lord God of Host Elohim Tzaboath
Sons of Elohim=Bene Elohim
Mercury
Intellect **(KMT)**

9 ☾

Geb/Malkuth
Two Feet
Kingdom
God Adonai Melekh
Souls of Fire=Ishim
(Alt) Female Generative System
Elements
Electromagnetic, Molecular
Body **(KMT)**

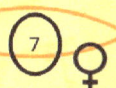
7 ♀

Het-Heru/Netzach
Right Leg
Victory South
God of Host Yehovah Tzaboath
Godly Beings=Elohim
Venus
Imagination **(KMT)**

10

Auset/Yesod
Foundation Below
Omnipotent Shaddai, EL Chai
Strong Ones=Cherubim
(Alt) Male Generative System
Moon
Reprogramming **(KMT)**

Rastafari Livity

− Receptive Female   **+ Active Male**

1

Crown Above
Obatala
Omnipresent (KMT)
White
Sage, Basil
Gaviton/String Theory

3 ♄

Babalu-Aye
Omnipotent (KMT)
Indigo, Black
Myrrh, Sypress

2

Ifa/Orunmilla
Omniscent (KMT)
Blue/White
Lotus, Sweet Almond

COVENANT OF UNITY

THE THOUGHT

5 ♂

Ogun
Divine Justice (KMT)
Blood Red & White
Pine, Cedar Wood

4 ♃

Aja Chagullia/Aganyu
Divine Law KMT
Sky Blue, Yellow
Anise, Oak Moss

6 ☉

Heart
Shango/Jakuta
Will (KMT)
Red & White
Olibanum, Geranium
Photon/Standard Model

8 ☿

Eshu/Elegba
Intellect (KMT)
Sophron Red, Black
Lavendar, Lily of the Valley
W/Z Boson /?

7 ♀

Oshun
Imagination (KMT)
Green, Yellow
Rose, Sandle Wood
Gluon/General Relativity

9 ☽

Yemaya
Electromagnetic, Molecular
Body (KMT)
Sea Blue
Spearmint, Jasmine
Higgs/?

71

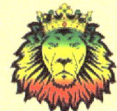

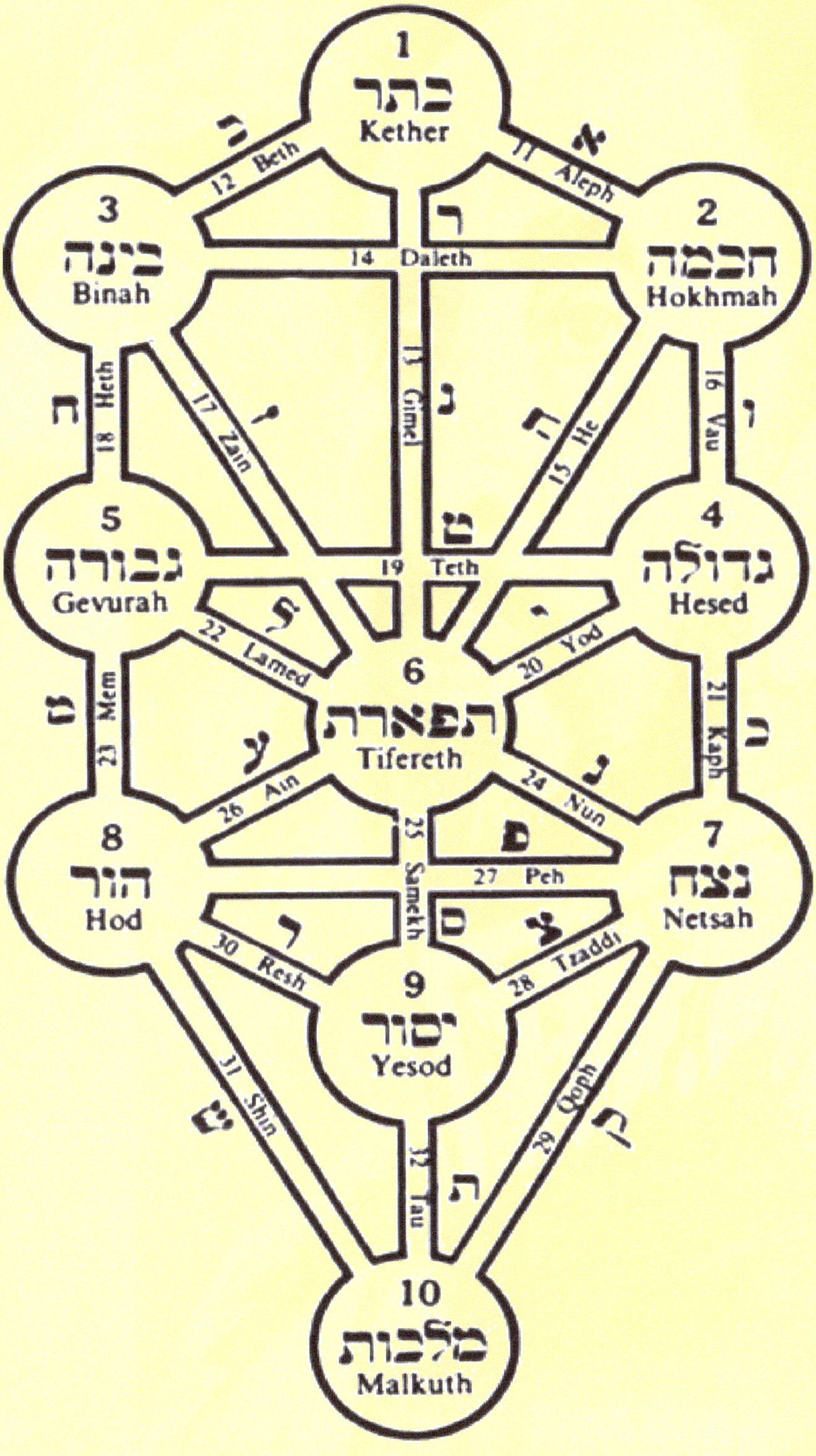
1
כתר
Kether
2
חכמה
Hokhmah
3
בינה
Binah
4
גדולה
Hesed
5
גבורה
Gevurah
6
תפארת
Tifereth
7
נצח
Netsah
8
הוד
Hod
9
יסוד
Yesod
10
מלכות
Malkuth
א 11 Aleph
ב 12 Beth
ג 13 Gimel
ד 14 Daleth
ה 15 He
ו 16 Vau
ז 17 Zain
ח 18 Heth
ט 19 Teth
י 20 Yod
כ 21 Kaph
ל 22 Lamed
מ 23 Mem
נ 24 Nun
ס 25 Samekh
ע 26 Ain
פ 27 Peh
צ 28 Tzaddi
ק 29 Qoph
ר 30 Resh
ש 31 Shin
ת 32 Tau

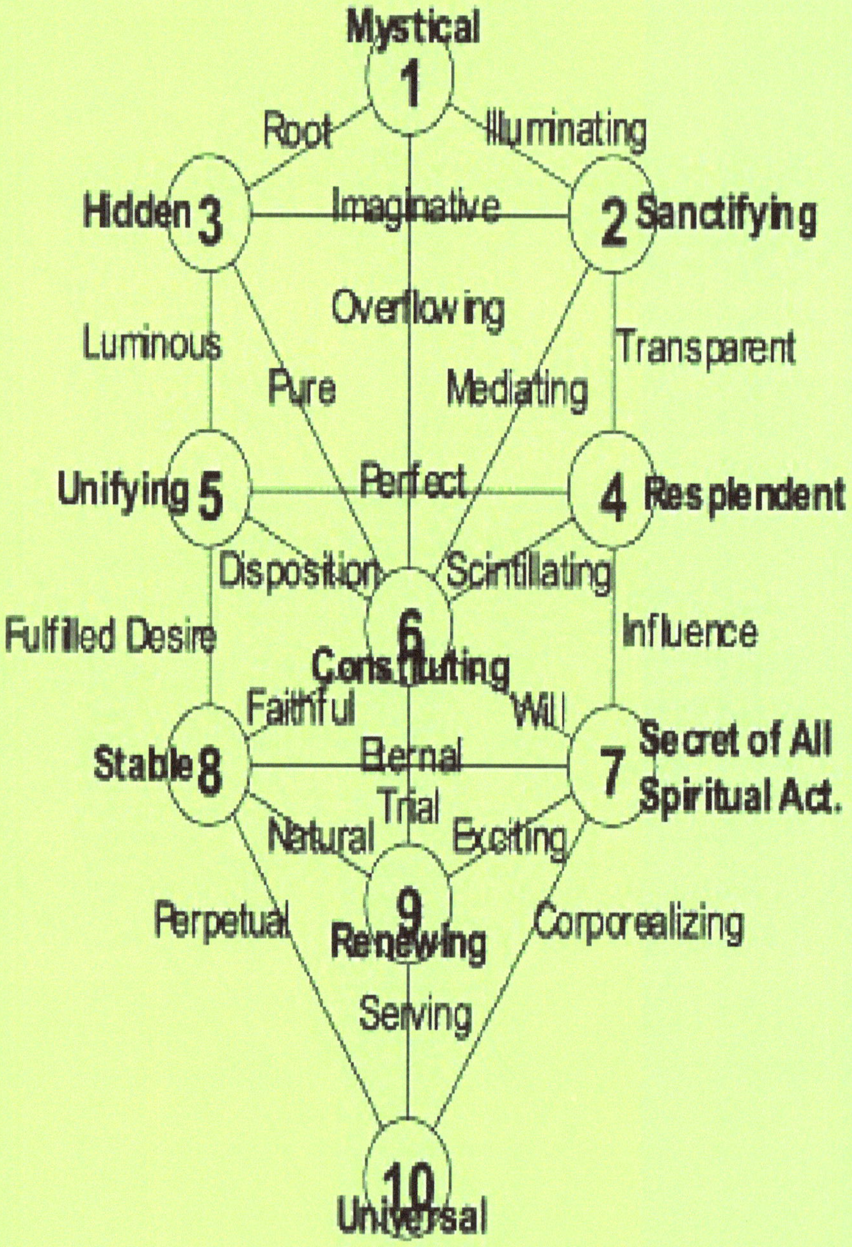

Rastafari Livity

Hebrew Paths

- 1 Mystical
- 2 Sanctifying
- 3 Hidden
- 4 Resplendent
- 5 Unifying
- 6 Constituting
- 7 Secret of All Spiritual Act.
- 8 Stable
- 9 Renewing
- 10 Universal

Paths: Root, Illuminating, Imaginative, Overflowing, Transparent, Luminous, Pure, Mediating, Perfect, Disposition, Scintillating, Fulfilled Desire, Influence, Faithful, Will, Eternal, Trial, Natural, Exciting, Perpetual, Corporealizing, Serving

 Rastafari Livity

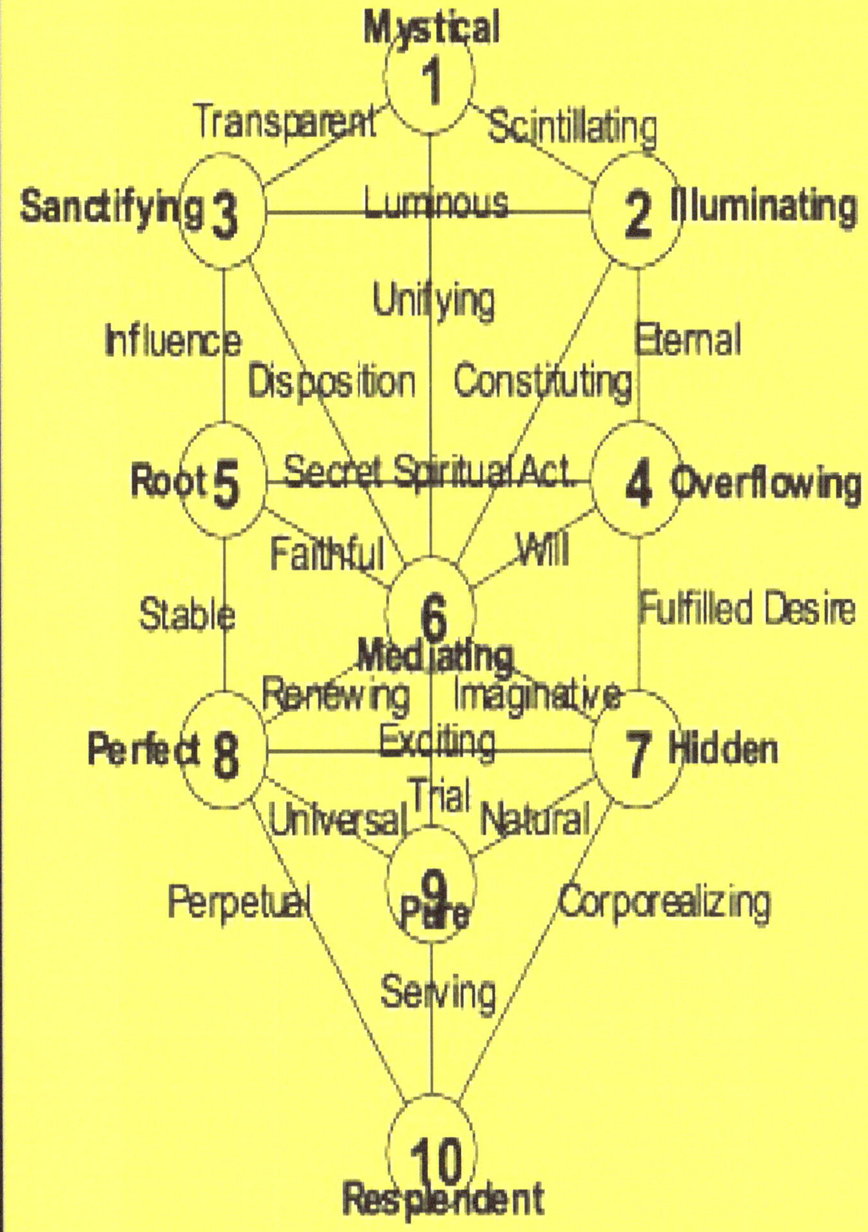

Western Hermetic Paths

- 1 — Mystical
- 2 — Illuminating
- 3 — Sanctifying
- 4 — Overflowing
- 5 — Root
- 6 — Mediating
- 7 — Hidden
- 8 — Perfect
- 9 — Pure
- 10 — Resplendent

Path labels: Transparent, Scintillating, Luminous, Influence, Unifying, Eternal, Disposition, Constituting, Secret Spiritual Act, Faithful, Will, Stable, Fulfilled Desire, Renewing, Imaginative, Exciting, Trial, Universal, Natural, Perpetual, Serving, Corporealizing.

Rastafari Livity

Chapter Nine

The Applicable Hebraic Element

After one of the Tree of Life Systems have become known, studied, Overstood and a part of InI's Life, InI continue to Omnify Rastafari, H.I.M. Hailie Selassie I, by listening, hearing, and doing what InI most Wonderful Queen taught, and spoke to Her Son, and Her People, at InI Hebraic Initiation. From the Kebra Negast (The Glory of The Kings): And the Queen said unto her Son, "My Son, God hath given unto thee the right, walk thou therein and withdraw not thyself from it, neither to the right hand nor the left. And Love thou the Lord thy God, for He is merciful unto the simpleminded. For His way is known from His commandment, and His goodness is comprehended through the guidance of His word."

Then she turned towards Elmeyas (the mouth of God, keeper of the Law, that is to say, keeper of Zion, and the Ear of the King in every path of righteousness) and Azariah (the High Priest of God) and all the mighty men of Yisrael saying, "Do ye protect him and teach him the path of the Kingdom of God, and the honor of Our Lady Zion. And whatsoever Our Lady Loveth not let us not do. Tell us truly and carefully forever and from generation to generation, so

Rastafari Livity

that she may not be wroth with us, if we do not perform her service well, so that God may dwell with us. And thou, my son, hearken unto the word of thy fathers and walk in their counsel. And let no drink make thee foolish, nor women, nor pride of apparel, nor the bridles and trappings of horses, nor the sight of the weapons of war of those who are at the head or at the rear. But let thy confidence be in God and in Zion, the Tabernacle of the Law of God, thy Creator, so that thou mayest vanquish thine enemy, and so that thy seed upon Earth may multiply..."

The Queen continued, and said to those of Yisrael, "At your words we will withdraw from that wherewith God is not well-pleased, and we will draw nigh unto every good thing wherewith God is well-pleased at your commandment. Only do ye instruct all this people, and teach them the words of knowledge, for never before have they heard such things as they have heard this day. It is only those who have understanding in them that wisdom and understanding illumine like the light of the sun..., ... I pray Thee, O Lord God of Yisrael, Thou Holiest of the Holy, grant unto me that I may follow wisdom, and may not become a castaway; grant unto me that I may make her a wall unto a foundation for me, and may never be overthrown; grant that I may stand upon her as a pillar, and may never shake; grant that I may hide in her, and never have her stripped from me; grant that I may build myself upon her, and may not topple over; grant that I may become vigorous through her, and not suffer from exhaustion; grant that I may stand through her, and may not fall; grant that I may lay hold upon her, and may not slip away; grant that I may grasp her firmly, and may not slide; grant that I may dwell in her in her peace; I may be satisfied at her table and may not vomit, and drink her and not get drunk upon her, and may be satisfied with her and not spit her out".

What the Queen prays, speaks, implies, connotes, and suggest is a never turning away from, neglecting duty towards, or failing in the Spiritual Awareness of InI Hebraic Element. She says what Menyelek must do, what the Kings after him must acknowledge, and what Rastafari is imbued within obligatory duty. This is a Sealed Covenant, because both King (Menyelek) and the Queen (His Mother Makeda) and all those who were round about, both small and great, "...bowed down and made obeisance...". Moreover, The Most High made them members of His House, for Zion was among them, and She is the Habitation of the Glory of The Most High. This Light of Inspiration shows that InI can add to InI duty towards The Most High, but InI can never take anything from InI duty.

Rastafari Livity

From King Solomon, through Emperor Menylek, H.I.M. and Rastafari receives the multipotent, multipurpose, multiseriate, and multispectral Ethiopian Hebraic Element for the function of exemplifying, **1)** That the lawful Kings of Ethiopia are descended from Solomon, King of Yisrael, through Queen Makeda; **2)** That the Tabernacle of the Law of God, i.e. the Ark of the Covenant, had been brought from Jerusalem to Dabra Makeda (Aksum) by Menyelek, Solomon's first born son, and Makeda's only son; and **3)** That the God of Yisrael had transferred His place of abode on Earth, from Jerusalem, to Dabra Mekeda (Aksum) the ecclesiastical and political capital of Ethiopia. These three begin the initiation of the Hebraic Element, but they are in no way the completion of it. The direction towards completion begins in the Priesthood of Zadok.

The descendants of Zadok the Priest, namely his first-born son Azaryas (Azariah), express the presence of the Hebrew Element in the form of the Priesthood. Azaryas (Azariah) brought to Ethiopia the surety of the presence of The Most High, being that The Most High had spoken to how "...these priests will continue to serve as My priests..." "They will come into My temple, where they will offer sacrifices at My Altar, and lead others in worship." Azaryas (Azariah) being anointed by Zadok, his father, the High Priest of Yisrael, to be the High Priest of the Kingdom of Ethiopia had with him, and read to the King and Queen of Ethiopia, "that writing which was written before God."

That Writing is the Laws, Commandments, teachings, instructions, and prophecies of the Hebrew Yisraelite Nation, InI's family. It was brought to InI because the separation of InI had taken InI from the Most High. There was a straying that required a straightening of InI course. King David, Emperor Menyelek, was perturbed when He discovered that The Most High had Blessed Ethiopia with His Return and Abode. It is written that the Emperor drew breath three (3) times at this news and awakening. Imagine, if you will, the state of mind in discovering that the Most High God has not forgotten you, even though you had forgotten Him, and has returned to you all because your spirituality had remained intact.

Rastafari Livity

Rastafari has to now draw InI three (3) breaths in fulfilling InI Spiritual Abstract Processing Ability. InI have to bring about a fulfillment in what is commonly known as Judeo-Christian to the Hebrew-Yisraelite-Orthodox Tewahedo Christianic Union. Rastafari must do this on the levels of education, intelligence, spirit, religion, and manifestation, in a coalescing system that's fundamentally and completely about One Love. That means that every aspect, and all viewpoints, point, direct, lead, and guides InI to Divine Love. Divine Love has to be imbued, suffused, embedded, infused, ingrained, and manufactured into InI cultural observation and perception. It has to become who and what InI see, and know of InI Selves.

The Hebraic Element gives InI multiple disciplines to apply in multiple areas of I Selves, so that InI can contribute a completeness in InI society. Every type, form, and existence of any interaction between all things have to be Overstood by Rastafari, so that the matter can be valued accordingly. The entirety of Life (which is all spiritual) should be known comprehensibly to Rastafari, in order to teach the operation in it successfully.

That means that InI must attempt to gain, and eventually conquer, Mind the Contrarious, take the position of Mind Actuating with Introverted Awareness, and express that introversion Holistically. When Introverted Awareness happens, that conscious subjective "I" forms, consciousness gains objectivity of self-forming "I Am", and soon thereafter, objectivity designs "Is", creating "I AM IS" Spatiotemporal. This Subjective Holism needs to be construed and proliferated throughout all levels, degrees, categories, classes, grades, and leagues; with networks of interconnectedness; diffused and layered upon every known, unknown, and imagined aspect of Life. InI must maintain an esurience to InI Divine Duty, never becoming complacent or appeased by any seeming successful result, knowing that there is an infinite amount of elevation accomplishable for InI.

The coadunation that makes up Rastafari is very unique in covering such a vast array of subjective Knowledge, Overstanding, and Wisdom. The connection of the diverse components is done through an engaging and renewing ability, rather than a disengaging and making different, but passing it off as a new, disability. How do InI engage and renew? Well throughout the

Rastafari Livity

aeons of history there has been only one way to properly worship the Divine Ultimate Spiritual Entity, and that way is to totally do it. So knowing this allows for the discovery of every element and component that's observable, and allow them to be admitted into any system, because either it was there already and was lost, or that it was there already and never revealed.

Rastafari is a Hebraic Israelite Order that is according to a Judeo-Ethiopic-Mystic Ideal. The Nazarite Vow, Mosaic Laws, and Tenets of the Orthodox Order, as defined by Ethiopian Tradition, are the elements of its construction. A non-flesh diet, prayer, contemplation, meditation, and fasting are all fundamental principles that are strictly adhered to. This strictness is measured against the practices of the Bahitawis (Nazarenes) of Ethiopia as a guide and is dutifully exercised. The two tenets of the Nazarite Vow of "...there shall no razor come upon his head...and shall let the locks of the hair grow; and also, "All the days that he separateth himself unto the Lord he shall come to no dead body" are adhered to literally and fervently. These two are the readily perceivable aspects that identify Rastafari. Under the Nazarite Vow, the idealized Rastafari doesn't cut InI hair, nor do InI eat or use anything that contains animal flesh or by-products derived from animals and/or their flesh. This includes eggs, which are the dead embryos of an animal, milk, and cheeses that are taken from and/or produced from the liquid of the bodies of animals. A pure Vegan status is Rastafari's dietary ideal.

The principle of fasting is the third readily perceivable aspect of Rastafari's identity. A Fasting is the single most prescribed component of Ethiopian Culture and is a commonality between all the different faiths. To Rastafari, fasting is ordained by JAH, and is an uncompromisable tenet to be exercised frequently. All Holy Days and Observances are preceded by a fast. Meals are to be taken or eaten only after the evening prayer is completed at sunset.

In Rastafari, as it pertains to Mosaic Law, the sacrificial and offering requirements are exercised with candles, incenses and fragrant oils, instead of

animals. Frankincense, Myrrh, Blue Nile, Sandalwood, Egyptian, etc. are a few of the many types of oils and incenses required for the daily, weekly, monthly, and annual holy tenets and requirements. The first thing to note, in the use of prayer and scented oils, in Rastafari, is that the entire body is anointed. From the top of the head to the bottom of the feet, oil is touched, rubbed or poured on so that the extensions of man, that carry out sin, are prepared as a sacrifice (i.e. offered, and asked to be cleansed from the use as tools of iniquity).

In Rastafari, JAH is within man, manifesting at times, and for circumstances, implementing Divine Justice. There is a Messianist Principle with a Millenarian Purpose. The way that this is comprehended is that man possesses within himself a divine attribute of either Priest or Prophet. To Rastafari, the Holy Trinity comprises of the three Spirits of Priest, Prophet, and King, in which Haile Selassie I, of Ethiopia, completed. Rastafari expects man's spirituality to permeate his days, behavior, speech, and activities, and be expressed in them. The Priesthood of Zadok, in the Ethiopian tradition, is cultivated in Rastafari.

Finally, as with all subjects that are studied and investigated, belief systems (religions) also evolve and ascend, due to new discoveries, and deeper, broader understandings, as defined by the belief system's ideal, over time. The study, exploration, and investigation of Rastafari, Ethiopia, and religion as a whole, by Rastafari, has revealed a Trimorphic Semitic, Ancient Hebraic, and Sceptering Judaic Essence, that is necessary for man's spiritual development. It has insisted the infusion of elements previously not known, and confirmed all components; thought by others to be foreign imports to Rastafari and non-existent in Ethiopia, but are exercised and practiced in Rastafari and Ethiopia. Rastafari emphatically exercises the practices and rituals, behaviors and activities, of the historical Yeshua (Jesus) as recorded in multiple holy and sacred texts; some previously not known by scholars of ancient times. Rastafari is a union of the ideals of Yeshua (Jesus) and Haile Selassie I, of Ethiopia. It is a Judeo-Ethiopic-Mystic Society. Rastafari takes historical and contemporary truths and carries out the whole duty of man, as it is applicable to religion and spirituality. Here-to-date, Rastafari is engaging in its devotion to the One God in a strictness that several historical councils, and the doctrines that came forth from them, have yet to place as requirements to believers and the faithful of

Rastafari Livity

One Holy God. Rastafari does what Yeshua (Jesus) did historically and what Halie Selassie I did prophetically, in His Kingly character. To Rastafari, it is paramount that the full personage of Yeshua (Jesus) and Haile Selassie I be taught and exemplified by believers and the faithful, and not just the agreements that were compromised by men at councils. We worship as first century Judaic worshipers of Yeshua (Jesus) did.

JAH's use by Rastafari is biblically confirmed in Psalms 68 K.J.V. Rastafari's theology is that we believe in the God of Abraham. The One God, Jah Almighty, maker of all that can be, both visible and invisible: and in the messianic traditions of a savior and redeemer, homoiousia with JAH ALMIGHTY, being His Imperial Majesty, Haile Selassie I of Ethiopia. Born from the lineage of King Solomon of Israel and Queen Makeda (Queen of Sheba) of Ethiopia. Monophysite as of His nature, hypostasis in identity. Revealed in the divine words of JAH, in His Holy Bible, in Psalms 2, 8, 16, 22, 23, 24, 40c 41, 45, 68, 69, 72, 87, 89, 101, 102, 110, 118; in 1st Timothy 6:15, and in Revelation 5, 11, 14, and 19.

Chapter Ten

Requirements for Rastafari

Requirements:

    Divine Inity is the Ultimate Requirement, so at all times, and in every race, anyone who Overstands Fearing JAH, and does what is Righteous and True, has been made acceptable to H.I.M. For by the Father's Will the Bridegroom comes down to her in the bridal chamber; that had been prepared. And he decorates the chamber with the Light of Beckoning, the Spirit of Elevation, and the Soul of Rastafari Livity.

    For JAH has Willed to make men holy, and redeem them. Not as individuals only, without any bond or link between them, but rather to make them into a Priesthood who will acknowledge H.I.M., and serve H.I.M. in Holiness. This is a marriage of the Soul, and is not like a marriage of the flesh; bound by man's laws. In this "Mystical Marriage" the authority in the confirmation is JAH. In a marriage of flesh (religion), those who physically combine can only do so temporally. When they do so they become satiated with the physical, and bring within themselves the antagonistic burden of physical

Rastafari Livity

desire. They can only assuage it, never fully eradicating it, because the flesh itself is a "Sempiternal Darkness". They eventually turn their faces from each other.

The marriage of the Soul is Divergence from the flesh. The joining here creates a "Single Life". Thus it has been said, "They will become a "Single Flesh". To Live with this Wisdom is "Rastafari's One True Requirement". For what man knoweth the things of a man, save the spirit of man which is in him? Even so, the things of JAH knoweth no man, but the Spirit of JAH. Now we have received, not the spirit of the World, but the Spirit which is of JAH; that we might know the things that are freely given to us of JAH as Spiritual Duty.

INI were originally joined to each other when INI was with the Father; even before any was led astray. The People of JAH are marked by characteristics that clearly distinguish INI from all other religious, ethnic, political, or cultural groups, found in history. This marriage has brought them together, again, and their Souls have joined their "True Love".

God is not the possession of any One people. But as JAH, He acquired a people for Himself from those who were previously not even considered people. In this, there is a gradual recognizing of INI Self, and "Joy" moves with a steady rise. No longer is the disgrace of "Widowhood" applicable; between flesh and Soul. INI adorn I Self with Knowledge, Wisdom, and Overstanding, Evermore; so that H.I.M. is Pleased to stay.

Made into "a Chosen Race, a Royal Priesthood", and a "Holy Nation", One becomes a member of this people not by physical birth, but by being born "Spiritually", and then "Mystically". INI have risen from "Sleep" and perceives H.I.M.'s Grace. Being Strengthen, Rastafari has reached for, and connected to, H.I.M.'s Energies. Entanglement has become INI State. Here and there is the constant merging for INI. A Wave of Continuous Flowing Enlightenment is engaged in All Three Hundred Sixty Degrees.

JAH's People have for their Head His Imperial Majesty, Haile Selassie 1st, of Ethiopia. The "Anointed" King of Kings, Lord of Lords, Conquering Lion of the Tribe of Judah. Because of this same anointing, the Holy Spirit Flows from the Head into the body. This is the "Messianic People" of the "Third Millennium". This creates the foundation of Requirements for INI. And while Emperor and

Rastafari Livity

Empress were "Crowned" on the same day, INI will also be "Crowned in Livity" bringing balance and Inity into, and out of, Rastafari.

Spiritual Practices

What is required in Rastafari is a continuous amalgamation of Ancient Judeo-Ethiopic Tenets with Ethiopian Orthodoxal Tenets, of the fourth century, to bring forth a coalescing of worship.

Required Daily Observances

Prayer is done, with the anointing of the Locks with prayer oil, and the lighting of incense in the reminiscence of all Twelve Tribes of Yisrael, 3 times daily: 6am, 12 noon, and 6pm or sunset, in an Easterly direction or facing Ethiopia, while standing, being on knees, or prostrated. The chanting or recital of Seven Psalms are done after the evening prayer. All prayers can be carried out on a prayer rug, or mat while wearing a prayer shawl or tallith.

Required Weekly Observances

Two fasting days, Wed. and Fri., during daylight hours. Meals can be had as early as 2pm.

Sabbath observance: sunset Fri. to sunset Sat., which also includes a daylight fast, Candles, two (2) prayer oils (Frank., Myrrh, Blue Nile, etc.); incense (Frank., Myrrh, etc.); challah bread (no egg); tea and/or juice (from a fruit not vine).

The first of observances for the week are the two fasting days that are according to the Orthodox Order, and are obligatory. Wednesday is a fast day because it is held as the day that the council conspired to crucify Yeshua (Jesus). Friday is a fast day because it is held as the day that Yeshua (Jesus) was indeed crucified. All meals must be eaten after sunset. Prayers, contemplation, meditation and scripture reading are carried out during the daylight fasting hours. These are done with the anointing of the Locks with oils, the lighting of candles, and the burning of incense, in reminiscence of all Twelve Tribes of Israel, and should burn throughout the observance time. The fasts are concluded with the evening prayer.

The second of observances for the week is the Sabbath, which is strictly adhered to according to the Nazarite Vow, within Mosaic Law, of the Biet Israel of Ethiopia. Preparation for the Sabbath begins on Friday afternoon, with the

Rastafari Livity

washing of the body and clothing. Food is made ready for two days, for there is no cooking or preparing of a meal allowed; all creative work is prohibited. The meal must be one that is vegan, including the Challahs, with no flesh or animal by-products. The drink cannot be wine, or any juice derived from the fruit of the vine. The drink must come from the leaf, bark, or fruit of a bush or tree. The Holy opening of Sabbath begins with the lighting of the Fire Key. It is either a wood or coal fire for an outdoor service. Two (2) candles are also included in the service. The two (2) candles represent the two (2) commandments of the Sabbath. The first is Zakhor, to remember, and the second is Shamor, to observe. Several Psalms are recited during the lighting: 68, 2, 83, 20, 11 and 9. Incense is then ignited from the flame and must burn continuously, with the Fire Key, throughout the service. Neither can be allowed to blow out or burn out. Next is the Nyabinghi, which is the beating of the drums (min. 3), with chanting and dance. This is to commemorate the first commandment of Zakhor, remember. There is then the recital of the Opening prayer, which is the union of Psalms 133 and the Rastafari Creed, that is taken from the Holy Piby. After this, the two (2) Beginning Challahs, teas, and/or juice are blessed and partaken of. This is the opening of the Sabbath.

The sevice of the Sabbath is begun with the reading of several Psalms 1, 121, 122, 123, 87 and 24. After the Psalms are read the Magnificence of God and His Creation is presented, or taught, in several different ways. It may be from holy scripture, ancient text, sacred commentaries, mystical teachings, music, video or the sciences. There is then a Reasoning about what was delivered to the House. The Sabbath service is concluded with Shamor (observe) meditation or contemplation. Challahs, teas, and/or juice are then blessed and partaken of, bringing an end to the Quddus Sebat Qen (Holy Sabbath Day).

Sabbath Nyahbinghi Heights

Sabbath Nyahbinghi begins with a spiritual stir of awareness of ease, rest, and peace. It's not just that a religious service or ritual is soon coming, it's the Sabbath Nyahbinghi for InI weekly observance, and perpetual benefit, that JAH ordained to be observed For-Iver. InI can feel the energy of the Sabbath approaching at the waning of the week's fourth and fifth days.

A mental purging begins that starts to compartmentalize InI issues, concerns, situations, and involvements. Whatever is realized, that can be solved,

Rastafari Livity

is given priority, and whatever is realized, that can't be solved is put away. Nothing lingers for InI into the opening of the Sabbath Nyahbinghi.

On the sixth day, all physical stresses and burdens are eased. All of the works that are considered physical exertions are carried out earlier in the day. Any activities that can't be completed will not even be begun; they will be put off until after the Sabbath. The rest that should be gained on this day of rest is total and complete rest; mind, body, and soul.

Anything that may be needed or required for the Sabbath Nyahbinghi should be bought or gathered up. Fire Key items like wood or coal, candles, incenses, oils, water, and sacrament are regular Nyahbinghi items and should be on hand. If there are individual or situational needs that require the attention, InI will be sure to attend to them. It's important to be very present and aware prior to the Sabbath Nyahbinghi.

The opening of the Sabbath is preceded by a purging, cleansing, and anointing of InI self. All articles of clothing are changed for Sabbath attire. In the purging, cleansing, and anointing, a meditation, prayer, and chant repetition is carried out; that purges the thoughts and concerns of this world out of InI focal conscious. All of InI attention and conversation is directed upon Spiritual and Mystical meanings of the subjects and objects of InI Livity for this week. InI anoint I self with oils and incenses to stimulate and enhance this experience. The different oils and incenses have different actions upon InI, and different purposes for InI, so InI choose them according to the vibes that InI am given from JAH RASTAFARI. With a drumming, a chant, and a prayer, the Sabbath Nyahbinghi is opened and sealed for InI to be immersed within it.

InI arrange the items of the altar and raise the Rastafari Flag. The Fire Key is lighted, and all of the items of the temple are lit from it (coal, incense, candles, etc.). The anointing oil of the Priest-King is offered to the Brethren and Sistren. This, at service ritual, is done so that InI can create the harmony of spirits for Nyabinghi. Each one is emitting their vibes of Sabbath and becoming in sync with each one. Once the heartbeat of the bass drum begin, InI will feel how this elevation is realized. The rhythmic swaying moves InI to that hum, and harmony is accomplished.

The altar is set with prayer and/or chanting. As each item is touched and moved, it is infused with the vibrations of the Word Sound Power that is emitting from the Heart of the Priest-King setting it. A Priest-King may have one prayer or

Rastafari Livity

chant, or a prayer or chant for each item, groupings, movements, or order, in which the altar is set. The heartbeat of the drumming assists in the solemnity and reverence that is given in the setting of the altar. One final Psalm or prayer is said once the altar is complete.

InI begin beating the drums to invoke JAH's Spirit into the Sabbath Nyahbinghi, and to ward off any wickedness before the opening prayer. Chanting, a Psalm, or many other spiritual exclamations, are voiced during this preparation Nyahbinghi. After a few moments, or when InI are in harmony, the drumming will wane for the opening prayer. The beating of the drums will get softer, lighter, and slower until there is a peace and silence.

InI prayer begins in Amharic, the proper language of JAH's people. InI may recite more than one prayer, in more than one of the other Semetic languages of Hebrew or Arabic. Ethiopia is the righteous residence to all the tenets of the Abrahamic Ways of Life from their ancient origins. JAH chose Ethiopia as the birthplace of humanity, as the nurturer of His Blessings, Mercy, Love, Spirit, and Truth, and as the ideal of the permeation of Spiritual Livity. Therefore, it is of the upmost importance that InI gratitude be spoken in InI Ancient Semetic Tongue. The Amharic language provides a means for expressing the Truth in the Spiritual Realm of ideals. Amharic ensures the proper concepts for thinking when spoken and heard. This inner knowing assists InI in problem-solving, and also helps InI regulate behaviors. A deeper cognitive development occurs through this sublime interaction.

Nyahbinghi drumming, chanting, and praising begins as the Priest-King concludes the opening prayer with the exclamation "JAH RASTAFARI, Almighty I, King Selassie I". Several of Rastafari's hundreds of chants are sung for the next few hours. This is a spiritual high-point time of thanksgiving and praise. JAH's Love, Mercy, and Power is observed intimately at these times.

There are times when Nyahbinghi drumming is the only thing done for the Sabbath Observance, and the others when a reasoning or teaching is brought forth. The Vibes determine what is done and how. There is minimal pre-determination of Sabbath Nyahbinghi, that way it is left to be purely spiritually guided; even in those rare moments of slight pre-determination of a subject, topic, or teaching. InI all have a "zone of proximal development" in InI Livity, where InI cannot solve a problem alone, but can be successful under the guidance or in collaboration with Elders, Brethren, or Sistren. This is

accomplished with the drumming and revelation or reasoning and elevation. JAH gives the direction.

The Drums

InI can sense the "Ancient" elevations becoming imminent as the drums are set. Mystical Energy is looming in I minds and hearts. InI Reality is altered trying to match the flow of the drumming. Initiated by I Spirit, InI become drawn into InI inner-selves as InI seek to overstand JAH's message that is being announced, by sound, into InI souls. Drumming raises InI "Morphic Frequency" and allows higher intelligence, that pulsate beyond this realm, to penetrate, and manifest InI Light.

The existence and use of the Drum is to maintain a link between InI and deeper, higher, more vast worlds. Africans, to this day, use it to invoke Ancestor communications and to enquire how to find ways to solve everyday problems. The entire concept of music nascented out of this form of communication; as InI have always sought a sound that InI can feel from the esoteric to the exoteric.

Repeaters and shakers play major roles in this rising. Along with chanting, they help to create the higher energy environment necessary for the Ancestors and higher intelligent beings to come through. High intelligence cannot survive in a low intelligence environment. InI Ancestors are high intelligent beings that need the appropriate stage to be set before they come forth from within InI.

There definitely needs to be a pause, a silence, to cleanse the frequency of InI environment and the thoughts within InI minds. InI need to feel the vibes of a coming, InI need to prepare for it.

The Drum is truly designed as a bridge between the worlds. Before the Drum is created, a ritual is performed on the animal that has been selected to have its skin used as the medium for communication. The Ancient African understood that InI are all light beings and as such can never suffer death, or be destroyed. The being within the animal is also regarded as light. The ritual performed is to ask the animal's light force dynamic aspect to go to the ancestral

Rastafari Livity

world, communicate with them, and then become a bridge between both worlds.

The animal's skin retains some of the energy of their light force dynamic aspect, and as such now gives InI a medium and connection to the inner world of InI Ancestors. The Drum is a living voice, with the striking of it now being heard in multiple worlds.

The aim is to raise InI frequency to the point where it can sustain the presence of InI Ancestors. The drumming speaks to the ancestral energies deep within InI, the singing is a calling of the ancestors to come forward from their realm within InI, to rise up, travel across our inner darkness and make themselves known in multiple forms of expression.

Some feel compelled to cry, some want to move with the growing energies inside, some close down mentally and have visions of past life memories or future probabilities, some feel overwhelmed and need to just sit, be silent, pause from life. Then there are those who can take it to the next level, raise their frequency, keep it raised, and allow higher intelligence to come through them to express themselves.

These ceremonies are conducted as part of a celebration, and on occasions when things are not going so well. In moments where rainfall (opportunity) has been scarce and where crops (resources) have not been so good. The elders recognized the Ancestors may need to be called to help find some answers.

At other times, these ceremonies are conducted as part of celebrations and occasions when things are well, very well. In moments where rainfall has been abundant (opportunities), and where crops (resources) have flourished. The elders recognized that the Ancestors needed to be thanked and given gratitude.

Rastafari Livity

Now, in today's time, InI need the drums and drumming more than ever. Our enemy has multiplied himself and his weapons, and the drums prepare InI and keep InI prepared for the Battle.

Required Annual Observances

Nyabinghi is an ancient African ritual of drumming, incense burning, anointing of Self with prayer oils (Frank., Myrrh, Blue Nile, etc.), chanting Psalms, prayers, praises, and invoking the divine presence in man to reveal itself, to manifest. This is done at the start of all services, observances, and programs; and on special recognition of days, events, people, and times (Astrological, celestials, etc.).

Orthodox Christmas January 7th, preceded by a forty (40) day fast that begins November 29th. It is a daylight fast that require meals to be eaten before sunrise and after 2 pm. Groundation Day, on April 21st, It's the observance of the visit of H.I.M. Haile Selassie I, of Ethiopia, to Jamaica. Leonard P. Howell, the first Rasta, birthday, June 16th. The nine-day ceremony starting November 2nd-10th consist of: Anointing with prayer oils, 7 differently scented, on the head, brow, and shoulders; a daylight, natural juices and teas, fast on 3,4,5, & 9th; vegetarian diet 6, 7th; total fast 8th, natural grains, fruits, and vegetables 10th; Reading 53 chapters of the Holy Bible; and prayers three (3) times daily (6am, 12pm, 6pm).

The first Sabbath of every month is a fast day. It is to be observed from sunset Friday to Sunset Saturday. Only the Blessed Challah can be taken in with tea and/or juice. Nothing else can past the lips on this day until after sunset Saturday.

Spiritual Holy Days

All of Rastafari Holy Days are preceded and observed by a fast. There is no observance without a fasting requirement. Every Holy Day requires, at minimum, a fasting during daylight hours. The Holy Days and titles of Rastafari is as follows:

(1) January/February= Shevat-Wamashi on the 1st of Shevat. Oriental Orthodox Christmas on the 7th of January. Preceded by a 40 day fast that begins November 29th.

(2) February/March= Adar-Fast of Esther 11-13 of Adar. Birth of Bob Marley on the 6th of February.

Rastafari Livity

(3) March/April= Nisan-Fast of Passover on the 14th of Nisan. Passover is 15-21, gad fat (feast) on the 22nd of Nisan. Preceded by a fifty-six day fast.

(4) April/May= Iyar-Second Passover is 15-21. Groundation Day is on the 21st of April. It's the visit of Haile Selassie I to Jamaica.

(5) May/June= Sivan-Harvest of the First Fruits and Shavuot (giving of Oit-Torah) on the 6th of Sivan. Bob Marley's transcending on the 11th of May.

(6) June/July= Tammuz-Fast is 1-10. For the destruction of Solomon's Temple. Birth of Leonard P. Howell on 16th

(7) July/August= Av-Fast is 1-17. For the destruction of the second temple. Birth date of His Imperial Majesty Haile Selassie I on July 23rd.

(8) August/September= Elul-Fast is 1-9. For the year rotates. Our Atonement on Elul 10th. Asartu Wasamantu on Elul 28th. Birth date of Marcus Garvey on the 17th of August.

(9) September/October= Tishrei- Blowing of Trumpets on the 1st of Tishrei. Yom Kippur (Day of Atonement) on the 10th of Tishrei. Sukkot is 15-21 of Tishrei. Ethiopian New Year is on the 11th of September.

(10) October/November= Cheshvan- Fast on the 1st of Cheshvan. For Moses seeing God. Reception of Moses by Israelites observed on the 10th of Cheshvan. Fast on the 12th of Cheshvan. Supplication is on the 29th of Cheshvan.

(11) November/December= Kislev-Harvest Fast on the 11th of Kislev. Shavuot (giving of Orit-Torah) on the 12th of Kislev. Coronation of Emperor Haile Selassie I on the 2nd of November, 9 days fast 2-10 of November.

(12) December/January= Tevet- Fast is 1-10.

The practices and requirements for all of the Holy Days are typical of the Yisraelite and are commonly known and described throughout the world. Only the frequent fasting and slight date variations differ, for they are of Ethiopic traditions. The dating of Rastafari Holy days, with the use of the Gregorian calendar, are due to the dates of the events being reported in the Gregorian

Rastafari Livity

time. This will be used until a better proficiency is gained in the Ethiopic calendar's structure and adjustments that differ from that of the Gregorian.

Religious Items

Personal Spiritual Items

Prayer and scented oils are of personal use in Rastafari. We use them to anoint our locks and selves. We know that to be anointed is to be made sacred (consecrated); to be set apart and dedicated to JAH, and to be divinely designated with enabling gifts of grace. This is a daily inauguration, and we know this subject is important to JAH because anoint, anointed, and anointing appears in more than 150 Spirit-inspired Bible verses, including 22 New Testament Scriptures. His Imperial Majesty, Haile Selassie I, of Ethiopia, coronation on Nov. 2, 1930, is where and when "anointing" continued to be a recognized necessity.

(1) Crowns. The Crown must be of the colors of red, gold and green dominance to black and/or without black in them.

(2) Prayer Rug/Mat

(3) Prayer Tallith/Shawl

(4) Prayer Oils- Frankincense, Myrrh, Blue Nile, Sandalwood, Egyptian, etc.

(5) Medallion- Star of David, Star of Solomon, Ankh, Orthodox Cross and their chains.

Congregational Spiritual Items

Prayer and scented oils are very important items of the congregation's need. Our faith is deepened, and we are enriched and brought closer to JAH as we understand the spiritual meaning, and use of exotic fragrances for prayer and praises, anointing our head, hands, and feet. JAH is obviously a lover of sweet-smelling fragrances and perfumes since those words (or forms of them) appear forty-one (41) and thirty-five (35) times in the Bible, respectively. Spices in the context of anointing oils, perfumes, and incense are mentioned throughout the Bible: 16 verses containing Frankincense, 17 with Myrrh, 5 with Spikenard, and

Rastafari Livity

many others featuring cinnamon, cassia, camphor, aloes, cedar, honey, mandrakes, pomegranates, lilies, and roses.

(1) Drums (min. 3) Bass, Repeater, Fundah

(2) Flag of Ancient Ethiopia

(3) Incense and Oils (Frankincense, Myrrh, Blue Nile)

(4) Coals (min. 2) wood or candles (min. 2)

(5) Pictures of Haile Selassie I

(6) Large Ankh

(7) Censer/Thurible

(8) Water Challahs and juice

Medical Prohibitions

No non-life preserving of life-saving procedures is used.

Dietary Standards

Strict Vegan according to the Nazarite Vow within Mosaic Law. No animal flesh in any state or condition is allowed. No animal by-products are allowed.

Burial Rituals

According to Mosaic Law

Literature

Black Man of the Nile and His Family
The African Origin of Civilization: Myth or Realty
Civilization or Barbarism

Rastafari Livity

Books of the Old Testament

1. Genesis	25. Reproof (Tegsats)
2. Exodus	26. Book of Wisdom
3. Leviticus	27. Ecclesiastes
4. Numbers	28. Song of Songs
5. Deuteronomy	29. Isaiah
6. Joshua	30. Jeremiah
7. Judges	31. Ezekiel
8. Ruth	32. Daniel
9. Samuel I & II	33. Hosea
10. Kings I & II	34. Amos
11. I Chronicles	35. Micah
12. II Chronicles	36. Joel
13. Jubilee	37. Obadiah
14. Enoch	38. Jonah
15. Ezra & Nehemiah	39. Nahum
16. Ezra II & Ezra Sutuel	40. Habakkuk
17. Tobit	41. Zephaniah
18. Judith	42. Haggai
19. Ester	43. Zachariah
20. Maccabeus I	44. Malachi
21. Maccabeus II & III	45. Book of Sirach
22. Job	46. Book of Joseph
23. Psalms	
24. Proverbs	

Rastafari Livity

Books of the New Testament

1. Matthew	19. Hebrews
2. Mark	20. I Peter
3. Luke	21. II Peter
4. John	22. I John
5. Acts	23. II John
6. Romans	24. III John
7. I Corinthians	25. James
8. II Corinthians	26. Judah
9. Galatians	27. Revelation
10. Ephesians	28. Canon of Zion Synod
11. Philippinas	29. Commandment of Synod
12. Colossians	30. Revelation of Synod
13. I Thessalonians	31. Canon of Synod
14. II Thessalonians	32. The Book of Covenant II
15. I Timothy	33. The Book of Covenant II
16. II Timothy	34. Clements
17. Titus	35. Didache
18. Philemon	

Rastafari Livity

Sacred Writings

The Kebra Negast, The Glory of The Kings

The Holy Bible of Ethiopia Orthodox with its eighty-one books.

The Holy Piby

The Holy Quran

Periodicals

The expositions and exegesis of Rastafari Brethren and Sistren.

Resources Material

(1) Ethiopian Book of Life

(2) Egyptian Book of the Dead

(3) Nag Hammadi

(4) Sefer Yetzirah (Book of Formation)

(5) Metu Neter I & II

(6) The Zohar Collection

Organization Structure

Decentralized

Rastafari Livity

Chapter Eleven

What is Man?

    Those who represent an ideal beyond the comprehension of the masses must be prepared to face the unrelenting persecution of the unthinking multitude; who are without that Divine Ideal which inspires elevation, creates progress, and stirs those rational faculties; which unerringly sift Truth from falsehood. The lots of Initiates, Sages, and Mavens, are therefore almost invariably unhappy ones.

    The world has ever been prone to heap plaudits upon its fools and calumny upon its thinkers. Only here and there do notable exceptions occur. For the most part, those that are ahead of their times in philosophy, religion, or science, are crucified, torn and rended limb from limb, burned, vilified, and if they're lucky, exiled by their opponents and/or society. Rastafari bears this same burden in these days and times. And with a duty towards "Righteousness", Rastafari is, and must remain, the inexpugnable leader, emblem, and High Priest of JAH Rastafari, Haile Selassie the First, of Ethiopia.

"What is Man, that thou are Mindful of him?"

Man's source of Being is the Supreme Incomprehensible Principle. Although indefinable, this "Absolute" permeates all of Space-Time. He is abstract to the degree of inconceivability, and is the unconditioned state of all things, substances, essence, or intelligences. He is the Most Ancient of Ancients. He is the "Circle of Life", itself emblematic, yet an Absolute Not-Being. He encloses a dimensionless area of incomprehensible Life, and the Circular Boundary of this abstract and measureless infinity. While InI postulate certain theories regarding the manner that He projects creation out of Hisself, using adjectives, nouns, and symbols, descriptive, in part at least, of His Powers, InI well know that to define Him is to defile Him. The "Only" True way to discover Him is through the process of eliminating, in order, all of His Cognizable attributes. That which remains, when every knowable thing has been removed, is InI Absolute "Source".

The "image and likeness" of JAH, that InI Am created in, is the Light of Conscious Awareness, Cognition, Self-Will, Discernment, Diversity, and Decision Making. These are the characteristics that InI have of JAH. InI also share the traits of Love, Mercy, Hate, and Judgement. These two, and their qualities, place InI nearer to JAH RASTAFARI than any other Creature of Creation. This is why InI Knowledge, Wisdom, and Overstanding also goes beyond the instinctual wants or capabilities of any other Creature of Creation. Man has a Uniqueness to his existence that is quantifiably greater than the rest of his family of creation, because "One-Third" of Man is JAH's Spirit.

... *"and the son of man that thou visitest him?"*

Man, unlike any other Creature of Creation, can also become, and is, corrupted in his soul body; the place where his mental and psychological characteristics and traits become subtle seeds and conscious manifestations. His characteristics and traits of the Most High JAH, that image and likeness that he inwardly possesses, can become duplicated, and that falsehood is then contaminated, soiled, or debased, in his soul, through his own efforts, non-efforts, or doings; or by the efforts, non-efforts, or doings of others that he allows into his Sphere of Influence, his Morphic Field.

Physical man is termed "dead" because, in the average individual, the Spiritual Creative Forces are limited in their manifestations in the purely physical form, and corresponding materialistic expression. Obsessed with the desire and belief in the Illusion of Permanence, in physical existence, man does not

correlate the material Iniverse with temporality, and that is his blindness, creating failure.

As the Solar Light is said to, symbolically, "die" as it approaches the Winter Solstice, so the physical world is described as being in the Winter Solstice of the Spirit. Reaching the Winter Solstice, the Solar Light stands still for Three Days, then begins its rise north, towards the Summer Solstice. The condition of ignorance may be likened to the Winter Solstice of Philosophy; and Spiritual Overstanding to the Summer Solstice with its high and bright Solar Light. Also, the Autumnal equinox, in which InI am now in, is analogous to the fall of man, at which time the human spirit descended into this realm of temporality by being immersed in the illusion of terrestrial existence. The Vernal Equinox of the Spirit in Man is beyond the realm of mortality, into that of Iternal Life.

Man was in the "Garden". He was placed in the Heights of Heights, the Levels Above, a Heaven in Similitude. He was in the midst of Supreme beings, sharing the Sphere of Wisdom and Overstanding. He was in the consciousness of his brethren, the Invisibles. But then came that Immersion, Man was put to sleep, which signifies a descent of rational, organized, supreme consciousness, into the illusionary, imaginative, impermanent realm of irrational, mortal ignorance. The Fall of Man signify our Spiritual Involution, simultaneously happening and parallel to our mortal, Emotional Conscious Evolution.

Man must now Overstand that his physical life, his temporal life, is likened to a great field of rich earth; out of which rises a myriad of plants, each different in color, formation, and fragrance, yet each with its roots in the same "Dark Energy"; which, however, is unlike any of the forms nurtured by it. He should Overstand that these "plants" are Iniverse, god, and man himself, that are nourished by the Supreme Absolute, and all having their source in that One Definitionless Essence. Everything, with their spirits, souls, and bodies, are fashioned from this Essence, and destined, like the plant in this analogy, to return to that Black Source, the Only Immortal, from whence all came.

"For thou hast made him a little lower than the angels, and hast crowned him with glory and honour."

The Ancients believed that the theory of man being made in the Image of JAH was to be understood literally. They maintained that the Iniverse was a Great Organism not unlike the human body, and that every phase and function of the Iniversal Body had a correspondence in man. The most precious Key to

Rastafari Livity

Wisdom, that the priest communicated to the initiates, was what they termed the "Law of Analogy". To the Ancients, the study of the Heavens was a sacred science, for they saw in the movements of the Celestial Bodies the Iver-Present Activity of the Infinite Father.

Man is the miniature world, an inner reflection of the vastness InI call Iniverse. Like an embryo, he is suspended, by all three (3) parts of the Triune Spirit, in the matrix of the Macrocosmic Energy. And while his temporal, terrestrial, body is in a perpetual Symphony with its mother Earth, his Astral Body lives in Inison with the sidereal "anima mundi". He is in it, as it is in him, for the world-pervading elements fill all space, and is the fabric of space itself, yet shoreless and infinite. As to his one-third of spirit, the Divine, what is it but an infinitesimal ray, one of the Countless Emanations proceeding directly from the Highest Cause- the Spiritual Light of the World? This is the trinity of organic and inorganic nature; the spiritual and physical, which are three (3) in one, and of which Proclus, the Greek philosopher and last major Neo-Plutonic teacher, says that "The first monad is the Eternal God; the second, eternity; the third, the paradigm, or pattern of the universe", the three (3) constituting the "Intelligible Triade".

Another philosophy describing man as "a little lower than the angels" is where the One Divine Nature of JAH manifests Itself in the threefold aspect of Father, Mother, and Child. These three (3) constituted the Divine Family, whose dwelling place is creation. God the Father is the Spirit of animation in all things; God the Mother is the matter and substance of all things; and God the child is the product of the two, represented as the sum of all living things born out of and constituting Nature. The Seed of Spirit is sown in the Womb of Matter, and by an Immaculate (Pure) Conception the progeny is brought into being. Such is the case with Nature Beings; they resemble neither spiritual creatures nor the material of their being, yet they are composed of the substance of both.

Rastafari Livity

Chapter Twelve

The Ancient Nyahbinghi Order
(Structure)

THE NYAHBINGHI IS OPENED WITH THE RECITING OF PSALMS, THE ROYAL PRAYER, RASTAFARI CREED, OR ITHIOPIAN ANTHEM.

THE RASTAFARI FLAG IS HOISTED AS PSALMS ARE RECITED.

THE NYAHBINGHI DRUMS ARE TO BE PLAYED BY CAPABLE RASTAFARI BRETHERN. A BALD HEAD OR NON-RASTAFARI IS NOT PERMITTED TO PLAY THE DRUMS. NO RINGS SHOULD BE ON THE FINGERS OR FIRE OF ANY TYPE NEAR THE DRUMS.

THE THREE DRUMS ARE:

1. THE BASS 2. THE FUNDEH 3. THE REPEATER.

THE BASS CARRIES THE TWO BEAT OR HEART BEAT IN ACCORD WITH THE FUNDEH THAT SAYS, "DO GOOD". THE REPEATER HITS THE NOTES IN ACCORDANCE WITH THE BASS AND FUNDEH.

Rastafari Livity

Priesthood

THE PRIESTHOOD OF NYAHBINGHI IS APPOINTED BY THE ESTABLISHED COUNCIL OF ELDERS ALONG WITH THE APPROVAL OF THE CONGREGATION.

THE PRIESTHOOD IS ADMINISTERED BY SEVEN (7) PRIESTS OF WHICH THE HIGH PRIEST IS THE HEAD. THEIR CONSISTENCY IN MAINTAINING AN IVINE LIVITY OVER A NUMBER OF YEARS MUST BE KNOWN.

ALL PRIESTS MUST POSSESS HUMILITY, KNOWLEDGE OF THE ORDER AND VERSE IN THE TEACHINGS OF HIS MAJESTY. THE OVERSTANDING OF SCRIPTURAL WRITINGS IS ALSO IMPERATIVE (ALONG WITH SCRIPTURAL MATTERS.)

THE PRIESTS CAN HAVE A QUEEN AS H.I.M. HAILE SELASSIE DOES, BUT SHE MUST BE ONE OF IVINE QUALITIES, ABIDING BY JAH LAWS. ALL PRIESTS MUST BE ONES OF JUSTICE WHO CARRIES OUT THEIR WORK WITHOUT PARTIALITY.

THEY MUST ALL MAINTAIN AN "ITAL LIVITY" MAKING SURE THEY DO NOT DEFILE THE TEMPLE OF THE LIVING JAH WITH ABOMINABLE FLESH.

THE PRIESTS MUST BE:

- SOBER IN BEHAVIOUR
- PATIENT
- HUMBLE
- RESPECTFUL

THE PRIESTS MUST NOT BE

- GREEDY
- GIVEN TO WINE
- A NOVICE
- DOUBLE TONGUE
- PRONE TO FILTHY LANGUAGE
- COVETOUS

THE NYAHBINGHI PRIEST MUST RULE HIS OWN HOUSE.

THE SIGNATURE OF THE HIGH PRIEST MUST BE AFFIXED TO ALL OFFICIAL DOCUMENTS OF THE ORDER OF THE NYAHBINGH TOGETHER WITH THE SEAL.

Rastafari Livity

A PRIEST WHO VIOLATES THE ORDINANCES OF HIS OFFICE AND THE NYAHBINGHI ORDER IS SUBJECTED TO DISCIPLINARY ACTIONS BY THE ANCIENT COUNCIL.

IT IS ADVISABLE THAT ONE AMONG THE PRIESTHOOD BE LEGALLY CERTIFIED AS A NOTARY OR AN EQUIVALENT.

CONCERNING THE FIRE KEY

THE FIRE KEY IS LIGHTED WITH THE READING OR RECITING OF SEVEN Psalms: NAMELY

(1) Psalm 101, which will be repeated by all, (2) Psalms 68, (3) Psalm 2, (4) Psalm 83, (5) psalm 94, (6) Psalm 11, (7) Psalm 9

IT IS THE DUTY OF EVERY BROTHER TO PREPARE WOOD FOR THIS FIRE, WHICH IS A CONSUMING FIRE FOR ALL EVIL DOERS IRRESPECTIVE OF COLOUR, RACE, OR CREED.

NO GARBAGE, WASTE OR REFUSE SHOULD BE THROWN IN THE NYAHBINGHI FIRE.

THE FIRE SHOULD BURN UNCEASINGLY DURING THE DAYS OF THE NYAHBINGHI.

THE FIRE MUST NOT BE DISTURBED.

NO FOOD SHOULD BE COOKED OR ROASTED ON THIS FIRE AT NO TIME.

BOTH SONS AND DAUGHTERS CAN GATHER AROUND THIS FIRE FOR WARMTH OR TO POUR OUT THE JUDGEMENT ON MYSTERY BABYLON.

CONCERNING THE TABERNACLE

THE TABERNACLE CONSISTS OF TWELVE OUTER POSTS WHICH REPRESENTS:

- THE TWELVE PATRIARCHS
- THE TWELVE GATES OF NEW JERUSALEM
- THE TWELVE TRIBES OF ISRAEL
- THE TWELVE APOSTLES

Rastafari Livity

THE CENTRE POST, THE LARGEST OF ALL, REPRESENTS INI MAJESTY EMPEROR HAILE SELASSIE I WHO IS THE HEAD OF THE NYAHBINGHI ORDER.

THE ROOF OF THE TABERNACLE SHOULD TAKE THE SHAPE OF AN UMBRELLA, PORTRAITS OF H.I.M. DECORATES THE TABERNACLE.

NO WEAPONS, DRUGS, ALCOHOL, CIGARETTES OR TOBACCO ARE ALLOWED INSIDE.

NO OUTRAGEOUS BEHAVIOUR OR PROFANITY.

THE TABERNACLE MUST BE VIEWED BY ALL AS BEING ASSEMBLED AROUND THE THRONE OF JAH RASTAFARI HAILE SELASSIE I.

A TABLE OF FRUITS, HONEY, AND WATER CAN BE PROVIDED AT A DESIGNATED AREA OF THE TABERNACLE.

CONCERNING THE ALTAR OF THE TABERNACLE

THE ALTAR WHICH STANDS IN THE CENTRE OF THE TABERNACLE CONSISTS OF SIX OUTER POSTS SURROUNDING THE CENTRE POST OF THE TABERNACLE REPRESENTING:

- THE BOOK OF THE SEVEN SEALS
- SEVEN GOLDEN CANDLESTICKS

THE PRIESTS ADMINISTRATES AROUND THIS ALTAR WHICH IS LAID WITH AN ALTAR COVERING OF RED, GOLD, AND GREEN.

HERBS, PROPHECY, PORTRAITS, AND SPEECHES OF H.I.M. ARE PLACED UPON THE ALTAR. FLOWERS ARE ALSO USED TO DECORATE THE ALTAR.

THE NYAHBINGHI DAUGHTERS IF CALLED UPON BY THE PRIEST CAN APPROACH THE ALTAR TO DO AS REQUESTED. e.g. PRAYER, REPORT, SUGGESTION, ETC.

THE INNER SECTION OF THE ALTAR SHOULD NOT BE USED FOR A SLEEPING ROOM, BUT CAN BE USED FOR A LIBRARY OR STORING THINGS PERTAINING TO THE TABERNACLE.

Rastafari Livity

CONCERNING THE NYAHBINGH GROUNDS

NO FLESH SHOULD BE COOKED, BROUGHT, OR EATEN, ON ANY NYAHBINGHI GROUND, AS WELL AS THE USE OF ALCOHOL, CIGARETTES, TOBACCO, OR ANY ILLICIT DRUGS.

SEXUAL INTERCOURSE IS STRICKLY FORBIDDEN AND SELF DISCIPLINE MUST BE MAINTAINED.

STRANGERS ARE NOT PERMITTED THE USE OF CAMERAS UNLESS AUTHORISED BY THE HOUSE.

ALL HEADS OF FEMALES MUST BE COVERED AND THE WEARING OF

PANTS AS WELL AS EXPOSIVE GARMENTS IS FORBIDDEN.

ALL MEN MUST UNCOVER THEIR HEADS AT A NYAHBINGHI.

THE NYAHBINGHI GROUNDS CONSISTS OF A TABERNACLE, LION QUARTERS, LIONESS QUARTERS AND A KITCHEN (WHERE FOOD IS PROVIDED FOR ALL AT NO COST).

A STORE ROOM, AN OFFICE, AND SANITARY CONVENIENCES FOR BOTH MALE AND FEMALE ARE PROVIDED.

EVERYONE MUST BE PROPERLY ATTIRED.

WORKSHOP FOR ART AND CRAFTS AND SCHOOL FOR THE YOUTHS ARE VITAL STRUCTURES OF A NYAHBINGHI CENTER.

NO SICK PERSON SHOULD ATTEND AN ISSEMBLY.

ANY PERSON WHO IS INFECTED WITH ANY FORM OF CONTAGIOUS DISEASE IS NOT PERMITTED TO BE AMONG THE CONGREGATION.

NO SELLING OF HERB, OR OTHER ILLICIT DRUGS SHOULD BE CONDUCTED ON THE NYAHBINGHI GROUND/CENTRE.

LIVING, COMMERCIAL QUARTERS AND ANY OTHER DESIGNATED AREAS MUST BE APPROVED BY THE ANCIENT COUNCIL.

CONCERNING THE NYAHBINGHI SON (MAN)

THE NYAHBINGHI SON MUST ABIDE BY THE LAWS OF HIS IMPERIAL MAJESTY

HE SHOULD ABIDE WITH ONE QUEEN AS A PERFECT EXAMPLE SET BY HIS IMPERIAL MAJESTY EMPEROR HAILE SELASSIE I.

THE USE OF FLESH, DRUGS, ALCOHOL AND ALL HARMFUL ARTICLES OF FOOD MUST BE FORBIDDEN BY ALL. NYAHBINGHI MEN MUST BE NON- VIOLENT, NON-ABUSIVE AND NON-PARTISANT.

HE MUST BE FREE FROM ALL CRIMINAL ACTIVITIES, AS A TRUE SON OF H.I.M. HAILE SELASSIE I.

WHOREDOM, ADULTERY, FORNICATION AND SINFUL ACTS IS AN ABOMINATION TO THE MOST HIGH.

IT IS THE SOLE DUTY OF THE NYAHBINGHI MAN TO SEE TO IT THAT LOVE, AND HARMONY BE MAINTAINED AT ALL TIMES.

IT IS ADVISABLE FOR THE NYAHBINGHI MAN TO HAVE SEXUAL RELATIONSHIP WITHIN HIS ETHNIC GROUP. IF HE CHOOSES TO DO OTHERWISE IT'S A PERSONAL CHOICE.

A NYAHBINGHI MAN SHOULD NOT ABIDE WITH A WOMAN WHO IS NOT OF RASTAFARI LIVITY.

IT IS THE DUTY OF EVERY NYAHBINGHI MAN TO PROPERLY MAINTAIN HIS CHILDREN AND RAISE THEM IN THE ORDER OF RIGHTEOUSNESS.

EVERY NYAHBINGHI MAN SHOULD ACQUIRE A SKILL OR PROFESSION. IT IS WRONG FOR A NYAHBINGHI MAN TO TRIM AND/OR COMB HIS HAIR. THIS IS AN ABOMINATION.

THE NYAHBINGHI MAN MUST TREAT HIS FAMILY WITH LOVE RESPECT AND DEVOTION AT ALL TIMES.

HE MUST BE LOYAL TO HIS QUEEN IN ALL THINGS CONCERNING RIGHTEOUSNESS.

HE MUST BE ENTETERPRISING, CARING FOR HIS FAMILY AND NOT PRONE TO MISCHIEVE OR GOSSIP.

IF THERE IS A MISUNDERSTANDING BETWEEN HIM AND HIS QUEEN, THE MATTER SHOULD BE BROUGHT BEFORE THE PRIEST OR THE COUNCIL OF ANCIENTS, WHO WILL DEAL WITH THE MATTER PRIVATELY AND CONSTRUCTIVELY.

Rastafari Livity

TATTOOING OF BODY PARTS IS AGAINST THE WILL OF JAH. (HOWEVER, IF THERE ARE ONES WITH TATOO, THEY SHOULD BE COVERED, AND NO MORE ADDED).

CONCERNING THE NYAHBINGHI DAUGHTER

THE NYAHBINGHI DAUGHTERS, LIKE THE SONS, MUST ABIDE BY JAH IVINE LAWS.

AS H.I.M. IS THE HEAD OF THE NYAHBINGHI ORDER, THE NYAHBINGHI QUEEN MUST RECOGNISE HER KING AS HER HEAD.

DURING HER MONTHLY ISSUE, THE NYAHBINGHI QUEEN DOES NOT ATTEND, ISSEMBLE, OR CONGREGATE, AMONG THE BRETHRENS.

SHE MUST BE LOYAL TO HER KING HEAD IN ALL THINGS CONCERNING RIGHTEOUSNESS. SHE MUST BE ENTERPRISING, CARING TO HER FAMILY AND NOT PRONE TO MISCHIEF OR GOSSIP.

IF THERE IS A MISUNDERSTANDING BETWEEN HER AND HER KING MAN, THE MATTER SHOULD BE BROUGHT BEFORE THE PRIEST OR THE COUNCIL OF ANCIENTS WHO WILL DEAL WITH THE MATTER PRIVATELY AND CONSTRUCTIVELY.

DELICATE & SEVERE SITUATIONS SHOULD DEMAND PROFESSIONAL INTERVENTION.

A NYAHBINGHI QUEEN IS NOT PERMITTED TO PLAY THE DRUMS AT AN ISSEMBLY BUT IS PERMITTED TO THE USE OF THE SHAKA (SHAKER) OR TIMBREL.

DURING REASONING SHE CAN MAKE SUGGESTIONS AND PARTICIPATE IN GOVERNMENTAL ADMINISTRATIONS, AS IN THE TAKING OF MINUTES, WRITING OF LETTERS, OR ANY OTHER WORKS SHE IS CAPABLE OF DOING.

SHE MUST BE ATTIRED IN MODEST APPAREL AT ALL TIMES AND MUST NOT WEAR PANTS OR EXPOSIVE GARMENTS.

HER HEAD MUST BE COVERED DURING AN ISSEMBLE OR WHEN CONGREGATING AMONG BRETHRENS OR OUTSIDE HER GATES.

DURING AN ISSEMBLY, THE DAUGHTERS ARE RESPONSIBLE FOR THE TEACHING OF THE CHILDREN WITH SPECIAL EMPHASIS ON THE AMHARIC

Rastafari Livity

LANGUAGES, THE TEACHINGS OF HIS MAJESTY HAILE SELASSIE I, BLACK HISTORY AND OTHER ASPECTS OF RASTAFARI IVINE LIVITY.

WHEN THE NYAHBINGHI QUEENS BRINGS FORTH A PRINCE, SHE SHOULD STAY AWAY FROM AN ISSEMBLY FOR A PERIOD OF THREE (3) MONTHS. IF SHE BRINGS A FORTH A PRINCESS, SHE SHOULD STAY AWAY FOR A PERIOD OF FOUR (4) MONTHS.

THE WEARING OF JEWELRY IS NOT FORBIDDEN BUT THE PIERCING, ALONG WITH TATTOOING OF BODY PARTS IS AGAINST THE WILL OF JAH.

THE PLAITING OF LOCKS IS FORBIDDEN AS IT IS WRITTEN IN THE BOOK OF 1 ST. PETER 3, VERSE 3 "WHOSE ADORNING LET IT NOT BE THAT OUTWARD ADORNING, LET IT NOT BE THAT OUTWARD ADORNING OF PLAITING OF THE HAIR"... BLEACHING IS ALSO FORBIDDEN.

IT IS ADVISABLE FOR THE NYAHBINGHI DAUGHTER TO HAVE SEXUAL RELATIONSHIP WITHIN HER ETHNIC GROUP. IF SHE CHOOSES TO DO OTHERWISE IT'S A PERSONAL CHOICE.

THE USE OF FLESH, DRUGS, AND ALCOHOL & ALL HARMFUL TYPES OF FOOD MUST BE FORBIDDEN BY ALL.

NYAHBINGHI DAUGHTERS MUST BE NON-VIOLENT, NON-ABUSIVE & AND NON-PARTISANT. SHE MUST BE FREE FROM CRIMINAL ACTIVITIES FORSAKING WHOREDOM, ADULTERY, FORNICATION & ALL SINFUL ACTS.

THE ADMINISTRATION CONSISTS OF:

- PRIESTHOOD
- COUNCIL OF ANCIENTS
- ADMINISTRATIVE COMMITTEE
- ILECT OF RECORDS
- ILECT OF TREASURY
- SISTERS COMMITTEE
- WORKING COMMITTEE
- DISCIPLINARY COMMITTEE
- WELCOME COMMITTEE

Rastafari Livity

THE PRIESTHOOD

THE PRIESTHOOD CONSISTS OF BRETHRENS WHO ARE WELL NURTURED IN THE IVINE LIVITY OF RASTAFARI AND HAVE LED EXEMPLARY LIVES IN THE SIGHT OF THE CONGREGATION AND OF THE ALMIGHTY. THE PRIEST LEADS THE CONGREGATION IN PRAYER AND MAINTAINS HARMONY IN REASONING SESSIONS. THE PRIESTHOOD ARE LOOKED UPON FOR WISE DECISIONS, COUNCIL AND ARE KEY REPRESENTATIVES OF THE NYAHBINGHI ORDER. THE SIGNATURE FROM THE PRIESTHOOD IS REQUIRED ON ALL COMMUNICATION SENT OUT FROM THE HOUSE.

THE COUNCIL OF ANCIENTS

COUNCIL OF ANCIENTS CONSISTS OF ANCIENT PATRIARCH, MATRIARCHS AND OTHER BRETHRENS AND SISTREN OF THE HOUSE WHO HAVE MAINTAINED THE LIVITY OF RASTAFARI OVER A NUMBER OF YEARS.

THEIR DECISION IS ALWAYS REQUIRED AND WHERE THERE ARE DIFFERENCES OF OPINIONS, THE COUNCIL IS CALLED UPON TO MAKE A RULING.

THE COUNCIL OF ANCIENTS FUNCTION AS THE GUARDIANS OF THE MOVEMENT AND THEIR DECISIONS ARE TREATED WITH GREAT RESPECT.

THE COUNCIL OF ANCIENTS TIME OF MEETING MUST NOT CONFLICT WITH THE MEETING OF THE GENERAL HOUSE AS THEIR PRESENCE IS ALSO REQUIRED.

THE ADMINISTRATIVE COMMITTEE

THE ADMINISTRATION'S AIM IS TO ENSURE THAT THE HUNGRY BE FED, THE NAKED CLOTHED, THE SICK NOURISHED, THE AGED PROTECTED AND THE INFANTS CARED FOR IN ACCORDANCE WITH THE TEACHINGS OF HIS IVINE MAJESTY HAILE SELASSIE I.

THE ADMINISTRATORS ARE OF THE CONVICTION THAT A GOVERNMENT WITHOUT MONEY IS LIKE A BODY WITHOUT A SOUL.

THE ADMINISTRATORS ARE ALSO WATCHFUL FOR ANY INJUSTICES IN THE EARTH AGAINST RASTAFARI SONS AND DAUGHTERS AND ACTS ACCORDINGLY TO THE DECISION TAKEN BY THE ANCIENT COUNCIL AND THE CONGREGATION.

Rastafari Livity

THE CONSTANT AGITATION FOR REPATRIATION AND LIBERATION IS ALSO THE ADMINISTRATORS RESPONSIBILITY AND THEY WILL KNOCK ON ANY DOOR TO ACHIEVE THESE GOALS.

THE MOTTO OF THE NYAHBINGHI ORDER IS "ALL FOR ONE - ONE FOR ALL" <u>WORKING IN THIS MANNER THERE WILL BE NO FAILURE</u>.

THE ILECT OF RECORDS

THE ILECT OF RECORDS WRITES, RECEIVES AND ANSWERS LETTERS OF THE HOUSE WITH THE FINAL APPROVAL FROM THE ANCIENT COUNCIL AND CONGREGATION. THE ILECT OF RECORDS ALSO TAKES MINUTES OF MEETINGS AND DOCUMENT IMPORTANT EVENTS WITHIN THE FUNCTIONS OF THE NYAHBINGHI ORDER. AT LEAST THREE BRETHRENS MUST BE CHOSEN TO ADMINISTRATE THIS OFICE AND THEY CAN CHOOSE ASSISTANTS, BE IT SONS OR DAUGHTERS. IF THERE IS A WORKLOAD. THE SIGNATURE OF THE ILECT OF RECORDS IS ATTACHED TO ALL COMMUNICATIONS.

THE ILECT OF TREASURY

THE ILECT OF TREASURY CONSISTS OF AT LEAST THREE (3) REPRESENTATIVES OF THE ORDER WHO ARE COMPETENT ENOUGH TO TAKE RESPONSIBILITY FOR THE HOUSE FINANCES.

THE THREE (3) REPRESENTATIVES OF THIS OFFICE WILL HAVE THEIR NAMES AFFIXED TO A BANK ACCOUNT WITH ANY TWO FROM THREE ABLE TO MAKE TRANSACTIONS WITH THE APPROVAL OF THE CONGREGATION AND THE COUNCIL OF ANCIENTS.

THE SIGNATURE OF THE ILECT OF TREASURY MUST ALSO BE ASSIGNED TO THE COMMUNICATION OF THE HOUSE.

THE TREASURY DEPARTMENT MUST BE INVOLVED IN FUNDRAISING ACTIVITIES FOR THE HOUSE AND MAINTAIN A WRITTEN REPORT OF ALL FUNDS.

THE SISTERS' COMMITTEE

THE SISTERS' COUNCIL CONSISTS OF SISTREN OF THE NYAHBINGHI ORDER OF RASTAFARI. THEY HOLD REASONING SESSIONS AND DISCUSS ISSUES AFFECTING RASTAFARI SISTERS, FAMILY LIFE, EDUCATION OF CHILDREN, HEALTH CARE AS WELL AS ANY OTHER ISSUES WORTHY OF BEING DISCUSSED AMONG THE FAMILY OF RASTAFARI.

Rastafari Livity

THE SISTERS' COUNCIL ALSO CONSISTS OF:

- CHAIRPERSONS
- ILECT OF RECORDS
- ILECT OF TREASURY

THE ACCOUNT OF THE SISTERS COMMITTEE FOLLOW THE SAME RULES FOR BANKING TRANSACTIONS, i.e. TWO (2) OF THREE (3) SIGNATURES.

THE SISTERS' COUNCIL TIME OF MEETING MUST NOT CONFLICT WITH THE MEETING OF THE GENERAL HOUSE AS THEIR PRESENCE IS ALSO REQUIRED.

IF THE SISTERS' COUNCIL AGREES UPON A PROJECT, VENTURES ETC. THEY MUST FIRST BRING THE MATTER TO THE ANCIENT COUNCIL AND THE CONGREGATION FOR APPROVAL.

THE WORKING COMMITTEE

THE WORKING COMMITTEE OF THE NYAHBINGHI ORDER CONSISTS OF BRETHRENS AND SISTREN WHO VOLUNTEER TO WORK TOWARDS THE ADVANCEMENT OF THE NYAHBINGHI ORDER.

THE COMMITTEE ORGANIZES FUNDRAISING PROJECTS SUCH AS BANQUETS, ARTS AND CRAFTS, FARMING, TRADING AND ANY OTHER BUSINESS SEEN FIT BY THE COUNCIL OF ANCIENTS, WHO ARE NOTIFIED ALONG WITH THE CONGREGATION.

THE DISCIPLINARY COMMITTEE

THE DISCIPLINARY COMMITTEE CONSISTS OF SONS AND DAUGHTERS OF THE ORDER WHO SEE TO IT THAT THE GUIDELINES ARE ADHERED TO ON ANY NYAHBINGHI GATHERINGS.

IF ANY INDIVIDUAL FAILS TO MAINTAIN HARMONY AND LOVE DURING THE DAYS OF THE NYAHBINGHI, THEN THE COMMITTEE WILL APPROACH SUCH INDIVIDUALS IN A QUEST FOR ONENESS.

IF SUCH INDIVIDUALS RESPOND NEGATIVELY, THEN THE MATTER IS BROUGHT BEFORE THE COUNCIL OF ANCIENTS WHICH WILL THEN MAKE A RULING ON SUCH INDIVIDUALS.

WITH THE FULL SUPPORT OF THE CONGREGATION, THE COMMITTEE NEVER RESPONDS VIOLENTLY, BUT CARRIES OUT ITS DUTIES FIRMLY WITHOUT PARTIALITY.

 *Rastafari Livity*

IF THE MATTER IS OF A CRIMINAL NATURE THEN THE SECURITY FORCE SHOULD BE CALLED UPON TO ACT.

THE WELCOMING COMMITTEE

THIS COMMITTEE IS CHARGED WITH THE DUTY OF ASSISTING BRETHRENS AND SISTREN WHO VISIT A NYAHBINGHI FOR THE FIRST TIME. IT COMPRISES BRETHRENS AND SISTREN WHO ARE WELL-KNOWN FOR TOLERANCE, HONESTY, AND POLITENESS.

IF STRANGERS APPEAR, THEN THE COMMITTEE WILL INVESTIGATE THEIR MOTIVES AND REPORT TO THE HOUSE WHICH WILL DECIDE WHETHER SUCH INDIVIDUAL STAY OR LEAVE.

CONCERNING THE SANCTIFICATION OF CHILDREN

AFTER A PERIOD OF THREE (3) MONTHS THE NYAHBINGHI SON IS ABLE TO ATTEND HIS FIRST ISSEMBLE TO BE OFFERED UP TO THE MOST HIGH JAH RASTAFARI.

THE NYAHBINGHI DAUGHTER IS BROUGHT IN DURING OR AFTER THE FIRST FOUR (4) MONTHS OF INFANCY.

BOTH MOTHER AND CHILD SHOULD ATTEND THE ISSEMBLY, AS AT THIS TIME PARENT'S VOW TO GROW THEIR CHILDREN IN THE ORDER OF JAH RASTAFARI.

THE NYAHBINGHI PRIEST AS WELL AS THE CONGREGATION OFFER PRAYERS AND CHANTS FOR THE ITERNAL GUIDANCE OF THE CHILDREN, AND AT THIS TIME JAH MOTHER AND FATHER ARE CHOSEN TO HELP ALONG WITH THE UPBRINGING OF THE CHILDREN.

A SANCTIFICATION CERTIFICATE SHOULD BE GIVEN TO PARENTS AFTER SANCTIFICATION BY THE ADMINISTRATORS.

LEGAL CERTIFICATION BY LAW SHOULD BE SOUGHT SO THAT SUCH A DOCUMENT WILL BE ADMISSABLE WHERE REQUIRED.

IF AFTER THE SANCTIFICATION OF SUCH CHILDREN, PARENTS SHOULD CUT THEIR LOCKS, THEN THEY WOULD HAVE BROKEN THE OATH OF SANCTIFICATION. THE COUNCIL OF ANCIENTS WOULD THEN INVESTIGATE THE MATTER TO FIND OUT THE REASON FOR SUCH VIOLATION.

Rastafari Livity

RASTAFARI SONS AND DAUGHTERS MUST NOT GROW THEIR CHILDREN AS NON-RASTAFARIANS AS THEY WILL BE HELD GUILTY OF SUCH WRONG DOING.

IF AFTER EIGHTEEN (18) YEARS, OR WHEN THE CHILD LEAVES THE FAMILY HOME, HE/SHE DEPARTS FROM HIS/HER COVENANT, THEN THE JUDGEMENT WILL NOT REST WITH THE PARENTS BUT UPON HIS OR HER OWN SHOULDER.

THE SANCTIFICATION

WHEN THE CHILD IS BROUGHT TO THE ISSEMBLY FOR SANCTIFICATION THE PRIEST OR ANCIENTS OF THE HOUSE ARE NOTIFIED, AND THE "HOUR" IS CHOSEN FOR SUCH SANCTIFICATION.

THE MOTHER AND FATHER OF THE CHILD WILL STAND TOGETHER WITH THE CHILD, WHILE THE PRIEST READS FROM THE HOLY SCRIPTURE, PASSAGES PERTAINING TO THE OCCASION, NAMELY:

- 1ST BOOK OF SAMUEL, CHAPTER 1-BIRTH OF SAMUEL
- JUDGES CHAPTER 13-BIRTH OF SAMSON
- PSALMS 127
- EZEKIEL 44: 15-31

AS THE PARENTS OF THESE CHILDREN, MENTIONED IN THE ABOVE PASSAGES, VOWED THAT THEY BE NAZARITE FROM THE WOMB, THE PARENTS OF THE CHILDREN TO BE SANCTIFIED MUST DO THE SAME.

AFTER THE READING OF THE SCRIPTURES THE PARENTS THEN GIVE THE CHILD AND HIS OR HER NAME TO THE PRIESTS; WHILE THE ANCIENTS OF THE HOUSE GATHER AROUND THE HOLY ALTAR OF THE TABERNACLE, AT THIS TIME NYAHBINGHI CHOIR BREAKS INTO
SOLEMN CHANTS.

- THE MOTHER OF SALEM
- LITTLE CHILDREN
- CLAP YOUR TINY HANDS
- JAH GOT THE WHOLE WORLD

AND ANY OTHER CHANT BEFITTING THE OCCASION.

THE CHILD IS ANOINTED WITH OIL OF OLIVE, FRANKINCENSE, AND MYRRH ON THE HEAD AND FEET.

 *Rastafari Livity*

AS THESE SOLEMN CHANTS CONTINUE THE PRIEST MAKE KNOWN THE NAME OF THE CHILD TO THE CONGREGATION AND HE/SHE IS PASSED FROM ONE ANCIENT TO ANOTHER WHO MOMENTARILY RECITES PRAYERS UNTO THE MOST HIGH JAH RASTAFARI EMPEROR HAILE SELASSIE I, FOR THE GUIDANCE AND BLESSINGS OF THE CHILDREN.

AFTER ALL IS DONE, THE ANCIENTS ACCOMPLISH THE PRAYER AND BENEDICTION, THEN JAH MOTHERS AND FATHERS WOULD IDENTIFY THEMSELVES AT THE REQUEST OF THE PRIEST.

THEIR RESPONSIBILITIES ARE MADE KNOWN TO THEM ENSURING THE SPIRITUAL, SOCIAL & EDUCATIONAL WELL BEING OF THE CHILD.

WHEN THERE IS MORE THAN ONE CHILD TO BE SANCTIFIED, THE SONS ARE DONE FOLLOWED BY THE DAUGHTERS. HERE THEN ANOTHER CHILD IS OFFERED UP ONTO THE MOST HIGH AND ALL THE CONGREGATION ASK FOR HIS/HER GUIDANCE AND BLESSING HENCEFORTH AND FOR IVERMORE.

HOUSE MEETINGS

THE NYAHBINGHI HOUSE MEETS EVERY FIRST AND THIRD SUNDAY OF EACH MONTH FOR GENERAL REASONING.

AT THESE MEETINGS VARIOUS TOPICS ARE DISCUSSED AND DECISIONS TAKEN.

THE MEETING IS OPENED WITH HOLA CHANTS AND PRAYERS BY THE PRIEST, FOLLOWED BY A SPEECH OF HIS MAJESTY AND THE OPENING REMARK BY THE CHAIRMAN

THIS IS FOLLOWED BY AN UPDATE BY THE ILECT OF RECORDS OF PAST REASONINGS, AFTER WHICH MATTERS ARISING FROM OLD AND NEW ISSUES ARE DISCUSSED.

REPRESENTATIVES OF THE PRIESTHOOD, ILECTS OF RECORDS AND TREASURY MUST BE PRESENT AT THESE REASONINGS AND IF THERE IS A NEED FOR INTENSIVE PLANNING AND WORK TO BE DONE, THEN THESE MEETINGS ARE HELD EVERY SUNDAY OR ANY OTHER SELECTED DAY.

CONTRIBUTIONS TO THE HOUSE TREASURY ARE RECEIVED AT THESE MEETINGS AND THE HOUSE RESERVES THE RIGHT TO DISMISS OR DISALLOW ANY INDIVIDUAL FROM ATTENDING THESE MEETINGS.

Rastafari Livity

DISCIPLINE, TOLERANCE, AND OVERSTANDING MUST PREVAIL AT ALL TIMES TO ENSURE PERFECT HARMONY.

EVERYONE HAS THE RIGHT TO MAKE SUGGESTIONS AND HAVE THEIR OPINIONS HEARD AT THESE REASONINGS, WHICH ARE OPEN TO ALL SONS AND DAUGHTERS, BUT ONE VOICE MUST BE HEARD AT ALL TIMES.

AS WORDS WITHOUT WORKS IS IN VAIN, THE FRUIT OF ALL REASONING MUST BE PROGRESSIVE WORK.

Rastafari Livity

Chapter Thirteen

Black Heights; The Science

"Science is Religion with Greater Accuracy".

Science fr. L. Scientia = Knowledge fr. Scient- (pres. Part of Scire = to know); Possession of Knowledge as distinguished from ignorance or misunderstanding: Knowledge as a personal attribute. Knowledge possessed or attained through study or practice.

It is a shame that this particular word has been hijacked for use by a certain group or demographic, and feared to be used by other groups and demographics.

Science is knowing, but it is a knowing that is applicable, workable, and practical. It is a knowing that should be commonly recognized by others. Even if the Science is new and profound, there needs to be a dutiful effort to produce that particular Science into applicable, workable, practical, common sense (Our fundamental ability to perceive, understand, and judge things).

Rastafari Livity

In making science useful, the society at-large becomes more educated and more literate. Therefore, solving more of its individual problems and concerns, and negating the over use of law enforcement.

But that's the goal, and I don't want to put the cart before the horse. So let's describe the how, what, and why.

InI exist in an Iniverse described contemporarily by mathematics. But which math, and how do InI make sense of that math? Although it is interesting to consider that the Iniverse may be the physical instantiation of all mathematics, there is a classic principle for restricting the possibilities of errors and wasteful conclusions; and that is that the mathematics of the Iniverse should be "Beautiful". A successful description of nature should be a concise, elegant, "Inifying Mathematical Structure"; consistent with InI experiences.

Hundreds of years of theoretical and experimental work have produced an extremely successful pair of mathematical theories describing our World. But these were first conjured by thousands of years of Spiritual and religions works. Is it a coincidence then, that theoretical and theology both began with Theo-, the Latin word for God?

The Standard Model of particles and interactions described by quantum field theory is a paragon of predictive excellence. General Relativity, a theory of gravity built from pure geometry, is exceedingly elegant and effective in its domain of applicability; and they both mathematically describe the biblical Genesis chapter 1. Any attempt to describe nature at the foundational level must reproduce these successful theories, and their religious counterpart. The most sensible course towards Common Sense Inification is to coalesce and extend them with as little new mathematical machinery as necessary, but a more expositional narrative.

The further InI drift from these experimentally verified, subjective or objective, foundations, the less likely that information or mathematics will correspond with Reality. In the absence of new experimental data, InI should be very careful accepting any sophisticated, or simple, constructions of already proven Truths. Only when they provide a clear simplification, should InI pair and Inite existing structures with what's possible.

The Standard Model and General Relativity are the best mathematical descriptions InI have of InI Iniverse. The Creation Story in the Bible, with a few

Rastafari Livity

inclusions of more ancient teachings that the Bible is constructed from, is the best exegesis InI have of InI Iniverse. By considering these Sciences and following InI Guiding Principles, we will be led to a "Beautiful Inification".

InI being is Sapient; therefore, InI are Sapient Sapiens, and knowing is a fundamental ability of InI Nature. InI can know any and everything, but InI have to go about knowing in the most natural way of knowing and that is with InI Reasoning Ability.

All people are born with the Capacity to Reason. The power of forming a good judgment and distinguishing the true from the false, which is properly speaking what is called good sense or reason, is by nature equal in all men. Human beings have this unique advantage over all other creatures because InI can reason. Therefore, to become rational, a person need only acquire an education that teaches a good method of reasoning.

Each person has a rational will, which makes it possible to make and carryout plans. Animals, by comparison, are slaves of their emotions.

This reasoning and rationality is the power that enables people to "see" mathematical truths just as clearly as they can see a hand in front of their faces by visual perceptions. But since visual perceptions only yield particular, or contingent, truths more is required. Hence mathematics and its simple axioms (self-evident truths), that move from one self-evident step to another, yielding absolutely certain conclusions: For every action force, there is an equal and opposite reaction force.

People, with their ability to reason, can figure out the best course of action in any emotional state, be it when they are afraid, angry, or in trouble. In addition, people can make themselves do the right thing, instead of doing what may seem easier or more appealing.

But, and this is a big "But", people do not always plan ahead, but often act on impulse; which can be attributed to inadequate education or a miseducation of malicious and machinational intent. But if nurturing and strengthening is brought to the Capacity of Reason, some will elevate beyond their condition and circumstance.

Rastafari Livity

From the dawn of any history, Man has had faith and belief in Divine Forces and energies that created the world, and everything in it. Today, most people still have faith, believe, and pray to a Higher Power, a Permeating Energy, or a Superior Consciousness. But, is there really a way to measure if such an entity is out there? Scholars haven't yet convinced a majority, observing behaviors, and scientist have not yet found the proof, convincingly, that God, or something like a god, exist and/or created all of this.

Recent research, study, knowledge, and information sharing, suggest that the truth may not be outside but inside, inside all of InI.

InI will get to what's inside of InI all throughout this writing. Now, let's also look at this Higher, Permeating, Superior Origin of All Existence and the Nothingness it nascents from.

The best theory InI have for what made InI Iniverse predicts that it isn't just supremely big, but actually infinite; going on literally forever in all directions. This is very abstruse, and even obscure, in a scientific and religious way.

"In The Beginning God..."

Genesis is a word that has a Greek origin, that stems from the word "gignesthai", meaning, to be born, or the origin, or coming into being, of anything. InI can pretty much discover and/or identify the birth or origin of almost everything and every substance in existence, except JAH. So how can something be explained from No-Thing? The philosophical Latin proverb says, "Nil Ex Nihilo"- nothing stems, is from, or is out of No-Thing. So how can God be from Nothing?

The "Theory of Mind" is InI ability to empathize with other people and imagine what it might be like to be in that other person's perspective; from a certain point of view. This ability separates InI from every other creature.

Man already possess a "Theory of Mind" at a very young age. By somewhere between 3 to 5 years of age, young children consolidate a human way of thinking about the world; that there are features of the world that they can directly grab a hold of. They learn how to bridge together the abstract and the analytical of this world; things like force, energy, and mental states. No other creature shares this ability.

Only Homo-Sapiens are capable of believing in JAH. Out of about nine billion other species on earth none can perceive a Divine Consciousness except man; because being able to perceive a Divine Consciousness requires the Theory of Mind. This ability of belief in the Divine comes from an aspect of the Theory of Mind that gives InI the ability to comprehend that other "beings" are thinking.

InI begin to see a clear indication that children, at about 7-9 years old, are really beginning to Overstand that supernatural entities are thinking about what they're thinking, Overstanding; and in some cases, that they may not know something, but that the entity can help them by sending some Heights or Visions or Messages.

InI must be able to Overstand, in a two-way communication with a hidden entity, that that Supernatural Entity also has a Theory of Mind, that It too is aware that InI have a mind, a mind hard at work also. And, as simple as this may seem to some, this is actually a fairly sophisticated cognitive achievement. It takes very developed intelligence to actually perceive communication and answers to prayers, chants, and meditations, and Rastafari feels that these answers are real.

InI define reality by what InI can see, hear, touch, taste, or smell. Inside the brain, these senses exist as electrical signals. For InI, the entire sum of all reality is contained in a bundle of electrical wiring inside of InI heads. Atheist argue that our Theory of Mind is assisted by our creative imagination in the formulation of the Supernatural, and that all that we so call "Believe" can be quantified in our neuro-activity.

Neuro-theology, a new branch of neuroscience that studies that effects of spirituality on the human brain, can give InI some strong evidence of this "quantify and apply" aspect brought up by Atheist. But, it will prove their conclusion is an error, and only reveal that there is an enormous, elaborate, network involved in "Belief", and that neurotheology is merely documenting an

aspect of this vastness through medical science. Neuro-theology gives InI a way of peering inside the brains of believers while they are in the midst of a spiritual religious ritual. This science uses the highest of high-tech brain-imaging devices called SPECT scanners.

One example of its capabilities was revealed in an experiment with a Presbyterian minister. At the height of a prayer connection with JAH, the minister was injected with a dye that migrates to the parts of the brain where blood flow is the strongest- the brain works in a particular way, the more active a particular part is, the more blood flow it gets; and the less active it is the less blood it gets. The brain scan during prayer showed increased activity in the Frontal Lobes and in the language area of the brain of the minister. In fact, scans showed that in the midst of prayer rituals from Muslim Imams to Tibetan Monks to Meditating Atheist there was an increased amount of blood flow. So, when a person feels deeply focused on their prayer, there is an increased activity in the focusing area of the brain. This area of the brain, the Frontal Lobe, is intensely active when InI hold Trueversations. It allows InI to speak and to listen.

In Judeo-Christian prayer, the Frontal Lobe activates just as it would in normal conversations. To the brain, talking to JAH is indistinguishable from talking to a person. In Buddhist meditation, where they're visualizing something, a change can be seen, and an increase in activity, in the visualizing areas of the brain (in Buddhist practice, the Divine is an Abstract Presence, not a person who is directly spoken to, but rather an Essence that can be visualized during deep meditation).

When Neuro-Theologists looked at the brain scans of Atheists (people who do not believe in a god of any type) it was found that even simple, quiet meditation produces none of the brain activity of believers. To an Atheist, JAH is unimaginable, unknowable, unperceivable (hence why no one should argue religion). But to the Spiritual, and even some religious, experiences of JAH are more than thoughts. They are living sensations, vibrations, and are just as tangibly real as anything else in this physical world that InI senses transmit.

All religions create neurological experiences that are as tangibly real as if JAH's Revelation physically existed in the world outside the brain. And, what if JAH only existed inside the brain? Does that mean that JAH is not real? InI brains are where reality crystallizes for InI. And that comes from InI minds, which connects with the Mind of JAH, as the Theory of Mind describes and defines.

Rastafari Livity

Expeditions into the depths of the Mind, asking how can JAH come from nothing, are revealing a lot of answers, and even more questions. But since JAH is inseparable from the way InI see the world, the search for Divine Truths should turn InI away from the celestial, and towards self; where JAH is woven into every fiber of InI being (remember image and likeness). So, maybe the Nothingness that JAH Exists from is only hidden because of the way InI think "Nothing" of InI Selves?

... "created heaven and earth"...

Science's theory of a Big Bang, a cosmic explosion on an unimaginable scale, is the most recognizable and agreed upon origin of InI Inverse. What sparked the Big Bang, or triggered the explosion though, is up for extensive debate, and has several theories (recent discoveries have revealed so much more evidence to InI Truths). Understanding the True Nature of the "Nothingness" that gave InI "heaven and earth" is perhaps the deepest most baffling conundrum in InI modern times. Learning a little more about the possibilities could satisfy some of that depth and ease some clarity into InI answers.

With an infinite Iniverse, even extremely unlikely occurrences are possible. In the Realm of Life, all things have patterns. How these patterns are arranged determines who and what InI are. Small patterns can be found closer in proximity to each other. But larger patterns require larger searches, especially if the large pattern is also complex, like InI original "heaven and earth" that JAH created. So, the bigger and more complex the pattern is, the further InI have to travel before finding a repeat, and in this case, the repeat is actually the original.

The matter InI see in the Iniverse is just a tiny fraction of two vast seas of matter and antimatter. They would have completely destroyed one another were it not for the tiny imbalance found between the sub-particles B and Anti-B mesons. Because of the slight difference in the decaying properties of the anti-matter, InI is left with matter, as InI know of it, today. But this is just a sliver of matter compared to the original amount at the Big Bang.

Rastafari Livity

A massive chaotic explosion alone doesn't seem able to create the smooth and uniform InI see today. InI Universe, according to physics, exploded from some-thing the size of a sugar cube. That means that InI would need approximately 10 to the degree of 85 tons of high-energy explosives to equate such an explosion. That would be a billion, of a billion, of a billion, of a billion, of a billion, of a billion, of a billion, of a billion tons of matter, which is beyond sense and sounds totally unbelievable. Now from that, and adding up all of the matter InI know of, InI is left with an Universe, with a "heaven and earth", that is 95% empty. So where is the rest of InI "heaven and earth"?

"Dark Matter" is a non-detectable substance that makes up most of the matter in the InIverse. Dark Matter is non-detectable because it does not give off, reflect, or absorb detectable amounts of visible light, radio waves, x-rays, or any other kind of electromagnetic energy. Astronomers have discovered it only through its gravitational effects. They do not know its composition.

Evidence of Dark Matter comes from observations of galaxies. These studies show that the mass of any galaxy is many times larger than the mass of its stars and other visible parts. Further evidence of Dark Matter's existence comes from studies of radiation left over from the Big Bang and measurements of the rate at which the InIverse is expanding. The results from studies like these indicate that there are more than thirty times as much Dark Matter as is visible matter.

Dark matter, a 27% composite of InI InIverse, is called "Dark" because scientists are much more certain of what Dark Matter is not than they are of what it is. This is always the case when scripture is proven in science and confirms what is written.

... "and Darkness was on the face of the Deep" ...

This "Darkness" is in no doubt partly Dark Matter, and that's not just a name thing. First, it is not in the form of stars and planets that InI see.

Rastafari Livity

Observations show that there is far too little visible matter in the Iniverse to make up that 27% required, revealing a mystery or mysterious entity. Second, it is not in the forms of dark clouds of normal matter, matter made up of particles called baryons. This is known because they would be able to detect baryonic clouds by their absorption of radiation passing through them. Third, Dark Matter is not antimatter, because the unique gamma rays that are produced when antimatter annihilates with matter is not seen. And finally, scientists have ruled out large galaxy-sized Black Holes on the basis of how many gravitational lenses they see. High concentrations of matter bend light passing near them from objects further away, but they do not see enough lensing events to suggest that such make up that mystical 27% that Dark Matter contributes to the totality of the Iniverse.

It is also calculated that some Dark Matter may consist of Massive Astrophysical Compact Halo Objects (M.A.C.H.O.'s) bodies made of ordinary matter. Since 1993, observations have provided evidence of MACHO's in InI so-called Milky Way Galaxy. It is suggested that 20% of the Dark Matter in the so-called Milky Way Galaxy consist of MACHO's and that the mass of the individual MACHO's is about half that of the sun.

Another calculation of many astronomers is that most Dark Matter is Cold Dark Matter, particles that moved much more slowly than light particles in the early Iniverse. These particles might be Weakly Interacting Massive Particles (W.I.M.P.'s) which would be much more massive than protons. Or, they could be axions, which would be much less than electrons.

So InI have a number, and its detection is done through the lack of detections. But since it is a part of "Nothingness" there should not really be much to say anyway. Now, let InI discover what the remaining 70% of "Nothingness" is.

Sir Isaac Newton realized that the Nothingness of space must be something gluing matter, of all forms, to the large world around it, in relative proportions. Space is "something", and that something influences how matter moves. It is true of sand, water in a bucket, earth's rotation, InI revolution around the Sun, and the spiral of InI so-called Milky Way Galaxy.

In 1915, Albert Einstein's Theory of General Relativity showed that Newton's idea of space being "something" was fundamentally right. Space, or as

Rastafari Livity

he reformulated it, Space-time, is a bendable fabric into which all the matter is woven. The space that fills every corner of the Iniverse, plays a constant game of tug of war with all the things in it; be they planets, water in a bucket, or a stack of papers. So, if empty space is not empty, and is not "nothing", then what is it?

We have very dependable evidence that space itself is and can be in several different energy states-lower, medium, higher- and we also have good calculations to believe that InI space used to be in a much higher energy state in the early Iniverse, and whichever the kinds of particles that could exist were different. Now, this early Iniverse, which produced the mysterious Big Bang, was unstably adverse and quickly decayed into a lower energy state that InI inhabit today; which contains InI kinds of particles that InI are made of. This space is a great rippling ocean of particle waves emerging and then canceling each other out. There exist ripples from trillions upon trillions of particles waves. The energy contained in that great rippling ocean is causing the Iniverse to expand. The expansion is also accelerating, which can only be explained by an energy density that is pervasive in space itself. Physicists call this "Dark Energy".

..." And the Spirit of JAH moved upon the face of the waters" ...

The mysterious celeritous quantity known as Dark Energy makes up nearly three-fourths, or about 70% of the Iniverse, yet scientists are unsure not only "what" it is, but also how it operates. This is always how the "Divine" reveals itself. In physical cosmology and astronomy, Dark Energy is a theoretical form of energy that permeates all of space and tends to accelerate the expansion of the Iniverse. Dark Energy, at this present time, is the most accepted theory to explain observations, that derive from the 1990's, that indicate that the Iniverse is expanding at an increasing rate.

Dark Energy is thought to be very homogeneous, not very dense, and is not known to interact through any of the fundamental forces, other than gravity. Isn't this equivalent of free will, individuality, and even an allowed reprobateness? No interaction means no interference, other than what InI draw upon I Selves, Grab-I-tee (Gravity).

Dark Energy is quite rarefied, therefore making it unlikely to be detectable in laboratory experiments. It is beyond InI five, and sometimes sixth,

senses. Reportedly, Dark Energy has a very profound effect on the Iniverse, because it uniformly fills otherwise empty space with whatever its miraculous composition is.

The acceleration expansion effect is sometimes labeled "Gravitational Repulsion", which is an inner conflicting or confusing expression. Nonetheless, even though the only force carrier that Dark Energy interacts with is gravity, and gravity is what forms the objects within InI Universe, it is the mystical way, unknown as it is, that Dark Energy compels gravity that triggers this "repulsion". Negative pressure does not influence the gravitational interaction between masses, which remains attractive, but rather alters the overall evolution of the Iniverse at the cosmological scale. This typically results in the accelerating expansion of the Iniverse; despite the attraction among the masses present in the Iniverse. And just to be clear, this energy is not just acting "on things" in the Iniverse, it is acting "on" the Iniverse and "everything" in it.

Rastafari Livity

Chapter Fourteen

Rastafari Prayers & Chants

Psalms 1

Blessed is the man that walketh not in the counsel of the ungodly, nor standeth in the way of sinners, nor sitteth in the seat of the scornful. ² But his delight is in the law of Jah, and in His law doth he meditate day and night. ³ And he shall be like a tree planted by the rivers of water, that bringeth forth his fruit in his season; his leaf also shall not wither, and whatsoever he doeth shall prosper. ⁴ The ungodly are not so: but are like the chaff which the wind driveth away. ⁵ Therefore the ungodly shall not stand in the judgment, nor sinners in the congregation of the righteous. ⁶ For Jah knoweth the way of the righteous: but the way of the ungodly shall perish.

Psalms 1 (Amharic)

Mesgun New Bekfawoch Mekr Yalhid, Behathianyochm Menged Yalkom, Bewoznyochm Wenber Yaltkemth. 2) Negr Gen Begziabeher Heg Des Yelwal, Hegunm Bekenna Belielit Yasbal. 3) Arsum Beweha Fesashach Dar And

 *Rastafari Livity*

Tetekelch, Ferewan Beyegizewa Andmetsth, Kethlewam Andmayeregef Zaf Yehonal Yemisrawn Hulu Yeknawenltal. 4) Kefawoch Andih Aeydlum, Negr Gen Nefus Thergo Andmiwesdew Tbiya Nachew. 5) Selzih Kefawoch Befrd, Hathiatnyochm Betsadkan Mahber Aeykomum. 6) Igziabeher Yetsadkann Menged Yawkalna, Yekfawoch Menged Gen Tthefalech.

Psalms 24

The earth is Jah's, and the fullness thereof; the world, and they that dwell therein. ² For He hath founded it upon the seas and established it upon the floods. ³ Who shall ascend into the hill of Jah? or who shall stand in His Holy place? ⁴ He that hath clean hands, and a pure heart; who hath not lifted up his soul unto vanity, nor sworn deceitfully. ⁵ He shall receive the blessing from Jah, and righteousness from the God of his salvation. ⁶ This is the generation of them that seek H.I.M., that seek Thy face, Oh JAH Rastafari. Selah. ⁷ Lift up your heads, O Ye Gates; and be ye lifted up Ye Everlasting Doors; and the King of Glory shall come in. ⁸ Who is this King of Glory? Jah Rastafari, the Lord Strong and Mighty, the Lord Mighty in Battle. ⁹ Lift up your heads, O Ye Gates; even lift them up, Ye everlasting Doors; and the King of Glory shall come in. ¹⁰ Who is this King of Glory? Jah Rastafari, the Lord of Hosts, He is the King of Glory. Selah.

Psalms 87

His Foundation is in the Holy Mountains. ² Jah Loveth the Gates of Zion more than all the Dwellings of Jacob. ³ Glorious things are spoken of thee, O City of Jah. Selah. ⁴ I will make mention of Rahab and Babylon to them that know me: behold Philistia, and Tyre, with Ethiopia; this Man was Born there. ⁵ And of Zion it shall be said, His Imperial Majesty is Born in Her: and the Highest Himself Shall establish Her. ⁶ Jah shall count, when He writeth up the people, that this Man is born there. Selah. ⁷ As well the singers as the players on instruments shall be there: all InI springs are in Thee.

Rastafari Livity

Psalms 101

I will sing of Mercy and Judgment: unto thee, O Jah, will I sing. ² I will behave Iself wisely in a perfect way. O when wilt thou come unto I? I will walk within I house with a perfect heart. ³ I will set no wicked thing before I eyes: I hate the work of them that turn aside; it shall not cleave to I. ⁴ A froward heart shall depart from I: I will not know a wicked person. ⁵ Whoso privily slandereth his neighbor, him will I cut off: him that hath an high look and a proud heart will not I suffer. ⁶ I eyes shall be upon the faithful of the land, that they may dwell with I: he that walketh in a perfect way, he shall serve I. ⁷ He that worketh deceit shall not dwell within I house: he that telleth lies shall not tarry in I sight. ⁸ I will early destroy all the wicked of the land; that I may cut off all wicked doers from the City of Jah Rastafari.

Psalms 121

I will lift up I eyes unto the hills, from whence cometh I help. ² I help cometh from the Jah, which made heaven and earth. ³ He will not suffer thy foot to be moved: He that keepeth thee will not slumber. ⁴ Behold, He that keepeth Yisrael shall neither slumber nor sleep. ⁵ Jah is thy keeper: Jah is thy shade upon thy right hand. ⁶ The sun shall not smite thee by day, nor the moon by night. ⁷ Jah shall preserve thee from all evil: He shall preserve thy soul. ⁸ Jah shall preserve thy going out and thy coming in from this time forth, and even forevermore.

Psalms 122

I was glad when they said unto me, Let us go into the House of Jah Rastafari. ² Our feet shall stand within thy gates, O Jerusalem. ³ Jerusalem is builded as a city that is compact together: ⁴ Whither the tribes go up, the tribes of the Lord, unto the testimony of Yisrael, to give thanks unto the name of the Lord, Jah Rastafari. ⁵ For there are set thrones of judgment, the thrones of the House of David. ⁶ Pray for the peace of Jerusalem: they shall prosper that love thee. ⁷ Peace be within thy walls, and prosperity within thy palaces. ⁸ For my brethren

Rastafari Livity

and companions' sakes, I will now say, Peace be within thee. ⁹ Because of the house of the Lord our God, Jah Rastafari, I will seek thy good.

Psalms 123

Unto thee lift I up mine eyes, O thou that dwellest in the heavens. ² Behold, as the eyes of servants look unto the hand of their masters, and as the eyes of a maiden unto the hand of her mistress; so our eyes wait upon the Lord Jah, until that He have mercy upon us. ³ Have mercy upon us, O Jah, have mercy upon us: for we are exceedingly filled with contempt. ⁴ Our soul is exceedingly filled with the scorning of those that are at ease, and with the contempt of the proud.

Psalm 133

Behold, how good and how pleasant it is for InI to dwell together in Inity! ² It is like the precious ointment upon the head, that ran down upon the beard, even His Majesty's beard: that went down to the skirts of His garments; ³ As the dew of Hermon, and as the dew that descended upon the mountains of Zion: for there Jah commanded the Blessing, even Life for Ivermore.

(Amharic)

Wendmach Bhbert Biqmthu, Anho Melekam New
Anhom Yamr New; Krass Ask Thim And Mifass
Ask Aron Thim, Blebsu Medrbiyam
And Miward Shetu New.
Bet syon Teraroch And-Miward And
Armenoim Thel New Biziya.
Igziabeher Brektun Heywetnem,
Ask Zelalem Azezolena.

Rastafari Livity

THE LORD'S PRAYER (TSELOT) AMHARIC (phonetic transcription)
Matthew 6:9-13

| ABBA-TA-CHIN HOY, | BE-SE-MAI | YE-MIT-NOR, |
| Father our O, | In Heaven, | Who Art, |

SI MIH   YE-KE-DES,   MENGIST   TIMTA,
Your (Thy) Name   Hallowed   Thy Kingdom   Come,

FI-QA-DIH   BE-SE-MAI,   INDE-HO-NECH,
Thy Will   In Heaven   As Be Done

IN-DI-HUN   BIM I-DIR   TI HUN,
Likewise   On Earth   Be Done

YEIL LET   IN JERA-CHI-NIN   SI-TENE   ZA-REY,
Daily   Bread   Our   Give Us   This Day,

BEDELA-CHIN-NIM   YI-QIR   BEL-LEN,
Wrongdoings Our   Forgive   For Us

ENG-NAM   YEBEDEL-LUNN   YIQIR   ENDE-MINIL,
We   They Who Wrong Us   Forgive   As We

ABETU-WODE   FET-EN-NAM   AT-TAAG-BAAN,
Towards   Temptation   Lead Not,

KE-KIF-FU   ADIN-NIN   IN-JEE,
Evil   Deliver   But,

MEN-GIST   YAN-TE   NAT-TIN-NA,
Kingdom   For Thine   And Is,

HAIL-IM   MIS-GA-NAM   LEZEL ALEM-MU,
The Power   Glory   Forever and All Years,

    AM-MEYN
    Amen

Rastafari Livity

BABA YETU (Lord's Prayer in Swahili)

Baba Yetu uliye mbinguni, jina lako litukuzwe; ufalme wako ufike, (uje) Mapenzi yako yatimizwe, Hapa duniani kama mbinguni. Utupe leo riziki yetu. Utasamehe makosa, Yetu. Kama nasi tunavyowasamehe waliotukosea. Usitutie katika kishawishi lakini utuokoe maovuni [K wa kuwa ufalme ni wako, na nguvu, utukufu, leo na hata milele.] Amina

Ethiopian Royal Prayer

Behold how good and pleasant it is for brethren to dwell together in Inity. It is like the precious ointment upon the head, that ran down the beard, even Aaron's beard, that went down to the skirt of his garments, *As* the dew of Hermon, and as the dew that descended upon the mountain of Zion, for there Jah gave I-n-I Blessings, even Life For-Iver more.

The Teachings of Rastafari Doctrine is unto them that knoweth not foolishness, but unto I-n-I that knoweth it is the Power of Jah Rastafari. Therefore, I-n-I pray in the name of the Father, the Son, and the Holy Spirit of creation. For as Jah was in the beginning so is He now and so shall He For-Iver Be. JAH RASTAFARI!!

Prince and Princesses shall come out of Egypt, Ithiopia shall stretch forth her hands unto Jah, Oh thou Jah of Ithiopia, thou Jah of Divine Majesty, Thy spirit come into I-n-I hearts that I-n-I dwell upon the path of righteousness. Lead I-n-I teach I-n-I Love and Loyalty on Earth as it is in Holy Mt. Zion. Endue I-n-I with Thy Wisdom, Knowledge, and Overstanding to do Thy Will. May Thy Blessings be upon I-n-I that I-n-I hungry be fed, naked be clothed, sick be nourished, age protected, and I-n-I infants cared for. Deliver I-n-I from the hands of I-n-I enemies, that I-n-I may prove faithful in these last days. When I-n-I enemies have passed and decayed in the depths of the earth, the depths of the sea, or in the belly of the Beast! Oh, give I-n-I a place in Thy Kingdom For-Iver and I-ver more. So I-n-I hail I-n-I JAH RASTAFARI, Almighty JAH RASTAFARI, Terrible JAH

Rastafari Livity

RASTAFARI, who sitteth in Holy Mount Zion, and Reigneth in the Hearts of All Rasta Man, Wombman, and Child. Oh Hear I-n-I and Bless I-n-I and Cause Thy Loving Face to Shine upon I-n-I Thy children, that I-n-I may be saved. So let the words of I-n-I mouths, and the meditations of I-n-I hearts be acceptable in Thy Sight, Oh JAH RASTAFARI, I-n-I Strength and Redeemer. JAH RASTAFARI!!

Ethiopian Anthem

The Ethiopian Anthem is chanted at the opening and sealing of all ceremonial occasions and gatherings, and at the hoisting of the Ithiopian flag.

Ithiopia the land of InI Fathers the land where Ras Tafari love to be, As the swift bee to hive suddenly gathers JAH children are gathered to thee, With InI Red, Gold, and Green floating over INI, With INI Emperor to shield INI from wrong, with JAH and INI future before InI, InI hail thee with shouts and with chants.

CHORUS

JAH Bless InI Negus, Negus I, Who keep Ithiopia free to advance. To advance with truth and rights, truth & rights. To advance with love and light, love & light. With righteousness leading InI Hail to I JAH and I King, I'manity pleading One JAH for us all. O Iternal JAH of all ages, Grant unto InI sons that lead. Thy wisemind is given to the sages when Blackman was sorely in need. Thy voice through the dim past has spoken, Ithiopia shall stretch forth her hands. By JAH shall all barriers be broken and Zion Bless InI Dear Motherland. Ithiopia thy tyrants are falling who smote thee upon thy knees. Thy children are heartically calling From over the distant seas. RAS TAFARI the great one has heard InI, JAH has noted InI sighs and InI tears. With the Irits of love JAH has stirred InI to be one all through the coming years.

Rastafari Livity

Raising of the Ark Numbers 10:35

"Rise up, LORD, and let thine enemies be scattered; and let them that hate thee flee before thee."

Selah

(Hebrew)

Ha-Reemaht Ah-Rohn Ha-Ko-Desh

Koo-Mah Yah-Wah

Vi-Yah Foo-Tsoo Oh-Yi-Veh-Kah

Vi-Yah-Noo-Soo

Mi Sahn-Eh-A-Kah

Mi-Pah-Neh-A-Kah   Selah

Lowering of the Ark Numbers 10:36

"Return, O LORD, unto the many thousands of Israel."

Selah

(Hebrew)

Ha-Nah-Khat Ah-Rohn Ha-Ko-Desh

Shoo-Vah Yah-Wah

Ree-Vh-Voht

Al-Feh-Yisrael

Selah

Rastafari Livity

50 QUESTIONS MOST COMMONLY ASKED ABOUT RASTAFARI
****

1) Who is Jah? Jah is the supreme personality of the God Head manifested in His Imperial Majesty Haile Selassie I.

2) Who is Marcus Garvey? Marcus Garvey is a prophet and a visionary who sought to liberate black people from oppression and bondage.

3) Where was Marcus Garvey born? St. Ann's Bay, Jamaica on August 17, 1887.

4) What was Marcus Garvey's most famous prophesy? To look to Africa where a black king will be crowned King of Kings for the day of deliverance is near.

5) Was there a black man crowned king? Yes, on November 2, 1930.

6) Who was this black king? His name was Ras Tafari Makonnen of Ethiopia, Africa.

7) Who is Ras Tafari Makonnen? This was the name of His Imperial Majesty before he was crowned Emperor and adopted his kingly name of Haile Selassie The First.

8) What does Ras mean? Ras is an Ethiopian title reserved for great leaders or noble men, meaning "The Head" or "The Way".

9) How do we know that this is the prophesied black king? The Bible states that the black king will be crowned from the kingly line of David; See Acts 2:29-30, Psalms 87, Revelation 19:11-16.

10) What is the meaning of Rastafari? Rastafari means literally" Head, He to be feared" but it also represents a conscious movement of oppressed people united against oppression, who have accepted this Black King as their Messiah.

11) Is Rastafari primarily a religion? No, it is a way of life-based on cultural and historical traditions as well as religious principles.

12) Where and when was His Imperial Majesty born? His Imperial Majesty was born in Ethiopia, Africa on July 23, 1892.

13) Is His Imperial Majesty any relation to Jesus the Christ? Yes, Through the line from King David through the union of King Solomon and The Queen of Sheba, Makeda, and their son Menelik The First.

14) Where and when did the Rastafari movement originate? In Jamaica in 1930

Rastafari Livity

15) Do all Rastafarians where "Dreadlocks"? No.

16) What is the Nazarite Vow"? The Nazarite Vow is a Spiritual Commitment to a Way of Life that is Predicated on the Knowledge, Overstanding, and Wisdom of the World's Spiritualities. It is Accompanied by a Vegan Diet and the growing of INI Locks continuously.

17) What are "Dreadlocks"? Dreadlocks are an expression of the strength in a man and the defiance of the so-called values of Babylonian Society.

18) Who were the first Dreadlock Rastamen seen by the Jamaicans? The African "Freedom Fighters" called the "Mau Mau" of Kenya, in 1953.

19) What role did Marcus Garvey play in the Rastafari movement? His quest to uplift the Blackman against oppression along with his vision and his Prophesies gave Rastafari it's beginning and focus.

20) Does Rastafari have a theology? Yes, it's based on the crowning of His Imperial Majesty and the purification of worship towards the Creator from Black people first but all others also. Its conclusion is that we are all gods in spirit, kings in the flesh, and prophets to the people.

21) What were some of Marcus Garvey's Philosophies? "One God, One Aim, One Destiny". All men are created equal and should live in harmony, filled with brotherly Love.

22) What was the name of Marcus Garvey's movement? The Universal Negro Improvement Association.

23) Where was the U.N.I.A. started? In Jamaica in 1914.

24) What was Marcus Garvey's greatest accomplishment? He is the first African in modern history to start and lead a mass movement which had a primary objective of repatriation of black people to Africa.

25) Why did Marcus Garvey go to America? Because of an invitation given by Booker T. Washington in 1916.

26) What is the Black Starliner? It is the name of one of the shipping companies founded by Marcus Garvey in the 1920's. The other was the Black Cross Navigation Service.

27) What was the purpose of the U.N.I.A.? To uplift and dignify black people in all walks of life.

Rastafari Livity

28) What role did the K.K.K. play in the Garvey movement? The K.K.K. endorsed the movement's plans by offering financial and other assistance to help send blacks back to Africa.

29) Who was one of the chief persecutors of Garvey and his movement? J. Edgar Hoover the then head of the F.B.I.

30) On what charges were Marcus Garvey falsely indicted, persecuted and imprisoned in Atlanta before being deported back to Jamaica? Mail Fraud.

31) What does Jah, God, and Allah Have in Common? They all refer to the same one supreme, divine, omnipresent power.

32) What does Nyahbingi mean? The heartbeat of the people in their cry for freedom through drumming and chanting. And death to all downpressors of people, black or white.

33) In what year did H.I.M. take over the leadership of the Nyahbingi movement in Africa? 1935.

34) Who are the Mau Mau? Black anti-colonial freedom fighters from Kenya who supported the Nyahbingi movement which called for death to all black and white oppressors.

35) What is the capital of Ethiopia? Addis Ababa.

36) In what year did Benito Mussolini attack Ethiopia? October 3, 1935.

37) How many Ethiopians were killed by the poisonous gas that was sprayed by Italy? Six million people, plus cattle and wildlife.

38) Who blessed Mussolini's planes before they departed on their mission to destroy Ethiopia and her people? Pope Pius XI.

39) What year did His Imperial Majesty make his appeal for help and delivered his prophetic speech? In 1936 at Geneva, Switzerland.

40) Which country offered its assistance by way of arms, ammunition, troops, money or even moral support? None.

41) How did these events influence the Rastafarian movement? They served to consolidate the unity of the Rastafari members against Babylon's racism, Tyranny, and merciless oppression, and to conjure up universal Love and support among poor people for Emperor Haile Selassie I.

Rastafari Livity

42) Who is Robert Nesta Marley? In short, Bob Marley, a Jamaican-born, Rastafarian, Dreadlocked musician who expressed the divine inspirations of Jah in music, speech, and action. He opened the hearing and senses of millions of people downpressed by the Babylonian system. He uplifted Black Pride, Culture, and Dignity.

43) How did Marley's music influence the movement of Rastafari? Before Bob Marley, the Rastafari movement was limited to Jamaica and other Caribbean Islands, but when Marley started to gain notoriety he started to teach, through music called Reggae, the teachings of His Imperial Majesty.

44) Where did Reggae music originate and by whom? In Jamaica by a Rastafari named Count Ossie.

45) What is Reggae Music? It is the heartbeat of the downpressed people.

46) Why is Rastafari Highly associated with Ganja? Rastafari Know that this herb, Ganja, has special healing powers and has been used as such by our ancient forefathers including King Solomon.

47) What sickness does Ganja cure? Asthma, glaucoma, tuberculosis, arthritis and assists in cancer therapy, among the most commonly known.

48) Do all Rastafari smoke Ganja? No.

49) Do Rastafari eat Pork or swine? NO, the swine (pork) is considered an unclean animal and Rastafari do not promote uncleanness.

50) Do Rastafari believe in the resurrection? Yes, but more in the way of continuality.

Rastafari Livity

Ethiopian Calendar

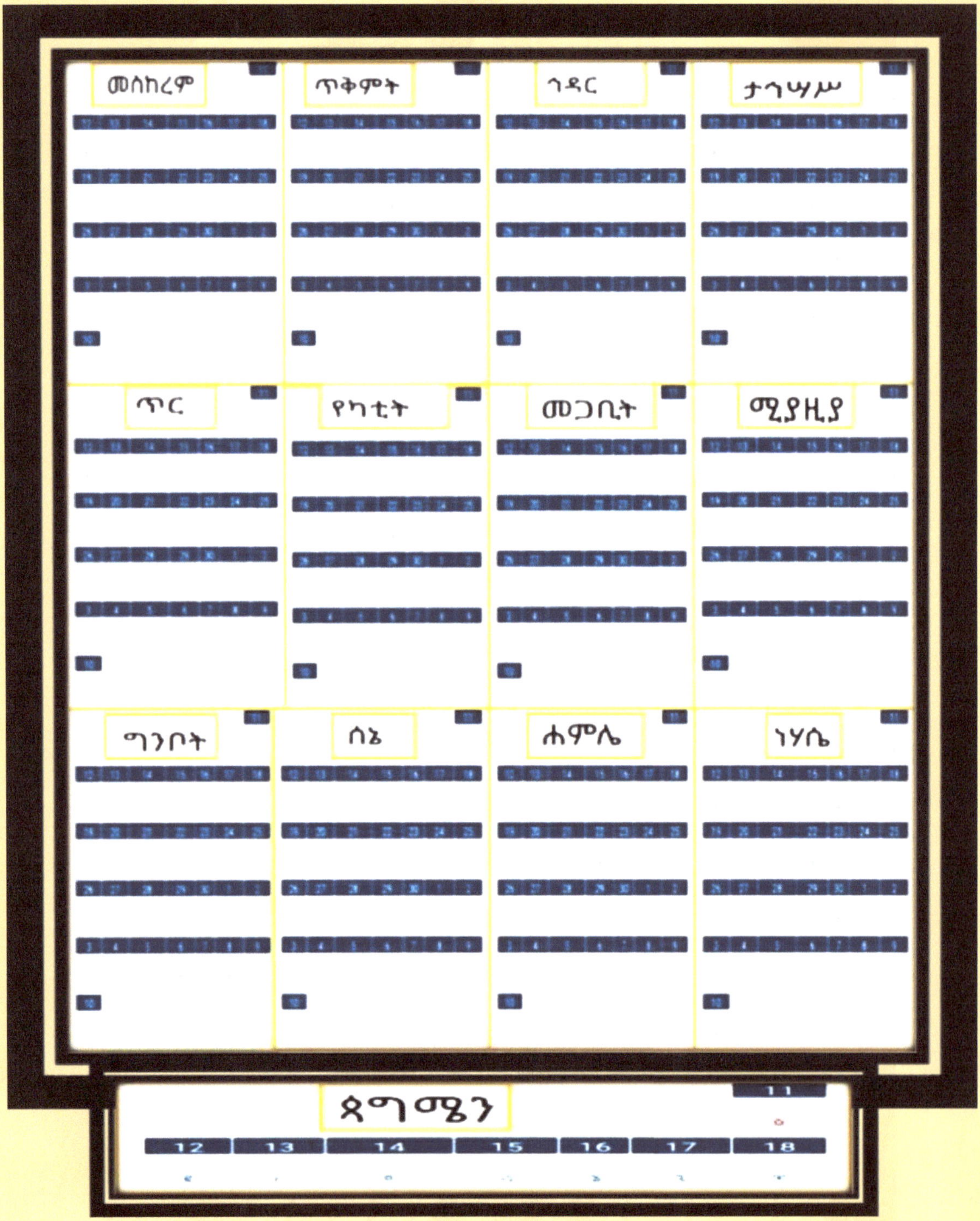

መስከረም	ጥቅምት	ኅዳር	ታኅሣሥ
ጥር	የካቲት	መጋቢት	ሚያዚያ
ግንቦት	ሰኔ	ሐምሌ	ነሐሴ

ጳጉሜን							
12	13	14	15	16	17	18	

Rastafari Livity

Ethiopian Alphabet

	ä	u	i	a	e	ï	o
h	ሀ	ሁ	ሂ	ሃ	ሄ	ህ	ሆ
l	ለ	ሉ	ሊ	ላ	ሌ	ል	ሎ
h	ሐ	ሑ	ሒ	ሓ	ሔ	ሕ	ሖ
m	መ	ሙ	ሚ	ማ	ሜ	ም	ሞ
s	ሠ	ሡ	ሢ	ሣ	ሤ	ሥ	ሦ
r	ረ	ሩ	ሪ	ራ	ሬ	ር	ሮ
s	ሰ	ሱ	ሲ	ሳ	ሴ	ስ	ሶ
sh	ሸ	ሹ	ሺ	ሻ	ሼ	ሽ	ሾ
q	ቀ	ቁ	ቂ	ቃ	ቄ	ቅ	ቆ
b	በ	ቡ	ቢ	ባ	ቤ	ብ	ቦ
t	ተ	ቱ	ቲ	ታ	ቴ	ት	ቶ
ch	ቸ	ቹ	ቺ	ቻ	ቼ	ች	ቾ
h	ኀ	ኁ	ኂ	ኃ	ኄ	ኅ	ኆ
n	ነ	ኑ	ኒ	ና	ኔ	ን	ኖ
ñ	ኘ	ኙ	ኚ	ኛ	ኜ	ኝ	ኞ
a	አ	ኡ	ኢ	ኣ	ኤ	እ	ኦ
k	ከ	ኩ	ኪ	ካ	ኬ	ክ	ኮ

	ä	u	i	a	e	ï	o
h	ኸ	ኹ	ኺ	ኻ	ኼ	ኽ	ኾ
w	ወ	ዉ	ዊ	ዋ	ዌ	ው	ዎ
a	ዐ	ዑ	ዒ	ዓ	ዔ	ዕ	ዖ
z	ዘ	ዙ	ዚ	ዛ	ዜ	ዝ	ዞ
zh	ዠ	ዡ	ዢ	ዣ	ዤ	ዥ	ዦ
y	የ	ዩ	ዪ	ያ	ዬ	ይ	ዮ
d	ደ	ዱ	ዲ	ዳ	ዴ	ድ	ዶ
j	ጀ	ጁ	ጂ	ጃ	ጄ	ጅ	ጆ
g	ገ	ጉ	ጊ	ጋ	ጌ	ግ	ጎ
t'	ጠ	ጡ	ጢ	ጣ	ጤ	ጥ	ጦ
ch'	ጨ	ጩ	ጪ	ጫ	ጬ	ጭ	ጮ
p'	ጰ	ጱ	ጲ	ጳ	ጴ	ጵ	ጶ
s'	ጸ	ጹ	ጺ	ጻ	ጼ	ጽ	ጾ
s'	ፀ	ፁ	ፂ	ፃ	ፄ	ፅ	ፆ
f	ፈ	ፉ	ፊ	ፋ	ፌ	ፍ	ፎ
p	ፐ	ፑ	ፒ	ፓ	ፔ	ፕ	ፖ

ALSO AVAILABLE

IF YOU ARE INTERESTED IN WRITING AND PUBLISHING WITH SOLOMON & MAKEDA PUBLISHING INC, VISIT US AT WWW.SM4PUBLISHING.COM